Startup CPO

A Field Guide to Scaling up Your Company's HR/People Function

Matt Blumberg and Cathy Hawley

Bolster Network

Contents

Foreword

Sott Dorsey

As a first-time tech founder and CEO at ExactTarget, one phrase kept ringing through my head: "I don't know what I don't know." Even with 10+ years of business experience and a freshly minted MBA degree, I had so many blind spots having never built software, raised venture capital or even led a multi-functional organization. Filling in these gaps took many years and lots of trial and error.

One of my gap-filling strategies was to learn from other CEOs going through similar highs and lows of scaling their company. On this journey, I was fortunate to meet Matt Blumberg. As CEO of Return Path, Matt was building a high growth company in the same digital marketing industry as me. I was impressed by his leadership, strategic thinking, and commitment to helping other entrepreneurs. We became fast friends and we both looked forward to learning from one another.

Matt was always gracious and willing to take my call or have dinner together. Our conversations covered every topic imaginable from leadership to board management to strategic partnerships to international expansion. My advice to entrepreneurs and leaders––build your peer network and spend time developing and nurturing these relationships. While board members and advisors are an important source of knowledge, learning from peers can be invaluable.

One of the highlights of my relationship with Matt was when we were both invited to the White House to witness President Obama signing the Jumpstart our Business Startups Act (or JOBS Act) in April of 2012. With bi-partisan support, the law opened up crowdfunding for startups and streamlined the IPO path. Exact- Target had just gone public two weeks prior so I knew the benefits that the JOBS Act would bring to entrepreneurs. But what I didn't know in April 2012 was that the event would foreshadow my relationship with Matt and how we would work together supporting entrepreneurs and startup ecosystems.

Fast forward to 2020. We are facing unprecedented challenges in the world and the need for innovation and leadership has never been greater. CEOs and functional leaders need tools and resources to accelerate their learning curves and the learning curves of those around them. Speed of learning, thought, and action are more important now than ever. This is why I am so excited about Matt's latest book, *Startup CXO*.

Startup CXO provides a comprehensive field guide to starting and scaling tech companies. Really, the information is super helpful to any company. It provides a "book within a book" framework to enable and empower readers to jump into any section as needed. And it's written by practitioners who provide tons of tangible advice and actionable insights. By reading this book, I believe that leaders will be better equipped to build great companies and anticipate what's around every corner.

In my view, the best CEOs have a grasp of all functions. They can go a mile wide and a couple inches deep. They hire A+ talent and build a culture that brings out the very best in people. They understand how Sales and Marketing fit together, they value HR, Finance, and Legal and understand their interdependencies, they have a clear vision for how Product and Engineering fit together, they know how to be aggressive and how to manage risk, and so much more.

So, *Startup CXO* is an amazing resource for CEOs but also for functional leaders and professionals at any stage of their career. The best functional leaders and professionals understand that cross-functional teamwork is everything. It's so important to have insight and empathy for how other areas of the organization operate. The big picture is needed to see how all of the puzzle pieces fit together.

I feel so lucky that through our venture studio, High Alpha, I have the opportunity to work with Matt and his leadership team as we build

Bolster––a talent marketplace for startup and scaleup tech companies. We are living and applying the concepts and lessons contained in this very book!

My wish for you is that reading *Startup CXO* minimizes your "I don't know what I don't know" list; that it accelerates your development, your curiosity, your ability to ask the right questions, and helps you surround yourself with the right talent. My wish is that you dream big, lead with purpose and integrity, and master your craft. I hope—and believe—that *Startup CXO* will be a helpful companion for you on your company-building journey.

Good luck!

Scott Dorsey
Managing Partner – High Alpha
November 2020

Update for 2024 Edition

I was delighted to hear that Matt and his leadership team at Bolster are breaking out *Startup CXO* into a series of enhanced mini-books to cover the "big 5" functions in a startup -- Finance, HR, Sales, Marketing, and Product/Tech. Each of these mini books provides the reader with a streamlined view of the critical elements of a single leadership function in a startup and highlights some of the best thinking around how to hire and lead teams. This book is power-packed with actionable insights that will serve as a valuable resource as startup teams scale.

Enjoy!

Scott Dorsey
Managing Partner – High Alpha
August 2024

Introduction

Matt Blumberg

In 2020 we sold Return Path, a company we had grown from a startup to over 500 employees over two decades. I documented the CEO journey in *Startup CEO: A Field Guide to Scaling Up Your Business*, but after publishing *Startup CEO* I was left with the nagging feeling that it wasn't enough to only help CEOs excel, because starting and scaling a business is a collective effort. What about the other critical leadership functions that are needed to grow a company? If you're leading HR, or Finance, or Marketing, or any key function inside a startup, what resources are available to you? What should you be thinking about? What does "great" look like for your function? What challenges lurk around the corner as you scale your function that you might not be focused on today? What are your fellow executives focused on in their own departments, and how can you best work together? If you're a CEO who has never managed all these functions before, what should you be looking for when you hire and manage all these people? If you're an aspiring executive, from entry-level to manager to director, what do you need to think about as you grow your career and develop your skills? And if you're a Board client or investor, what scorecard or metrics are you using to ensure your companies and investments are achieving greatness?

A number of my Return Path colleagues and I founded Bolster shortly after exiting Return Path and we started thinking about a new book as a sequel or companion to *Startup CEO*. That was the origin of *Startup CXO: A Field Guide to Scaling Up Your Company's Critical Functions and Teams*. *Startup CXO* ended up being a "book of books," with eight separate, detailed sections, one for each major function inside a company. Each section was composed of several discrete short chapters outlining the key playbooks for each functional leadership role in the company. Because it covered CFOs, CMOs, CPOs, etc.--we landed on "Startup CXO" as the name. As a field guide, *Startup CXO* was massive—over 600 pages and 132 chapters and while we think the content is relevant to the entire leadership team, we recognize that a more focused book on each function is also something people need. The result is the book you have here, *Startup CPO: A Field Guide to Scaling up Your Company's HR/People Function*, which is written for the current or aspiring Chief People Officer who wants to know how to scale their function, wants to know what "great" looks like, and wants to work effectively with other members of the organization. As an added benefit, this book is shorter, easier to carry, and cheaper.

While the content in this book is largely the same as *Startup CXO*, we updated it and added several chapters on "How to Hire a CPO," and "How I Work With the Leadership Team." We also moved the chapter on Fractional work from *Startup CXO* to this book so that all of the relevant CPO information is in one book.

One major change we should note is a reflection of society: when we wrote *Startup CXO,* the pandemic was just underway and neither us nor anyone else could have predicted the impact globally, much less the drastic impact on startups and entrepreneurship. The impact of the pandemic on the world of work, in how business is conducted is well-known, from the great resignation to the permanent remote work and hybrid models, but in the world of entrepreneurship the impact is less well-known. For example, in 2020 we wrote that "America's 'startup revolution' continues to gather steam" and noted that there are "increasing numbers of venture capital investors, seed funds, and accelerators supporting increasing numbers of entrepreneurial ventures." Today the world has changed, and while startup activity is still quite high, we are seeing more down-rounds, re-pricings, and recaps as venture capitalists are de-risking their investments. We're seeing expanding deal timelines and a focus on governance and accountability. Founders are likely to be operating under a microscope with less leeway, and with more scrutiny on management accountability and structures ensuring performance-based compensation. What that means for today's founders is that they need to develop a great organization right out of the gate, and that's where *Startup CPO* will come in handy.

While there are a number of books in the marketplace about CEOs and leadership, and some about individual functional disciplines (lots of books on the topic of Sales, the topic of Product Development, and the like), there are very few books that are practical how-to guides for any individual function, and that is where this series of "mini books" can help guide startup and scaleup teams. Each book in this series will serve as a how-to guide for a given executive, and taken together, the series will be a good how-to guide for startup executive teams in general. The five books are:

Finance and Administration
People and Human Resources
Marketing
Sales
Product and Engineering

We are starting with these "big five," but we may come back later and add to the series with Customer Success, Privacy, Business Development, and Operations, the other sections of *Startup CXO.*

This book carries my name as its principal author, and although I'm writing parts of it and editing it, I'm not THE author, I'm AN author. Cathy Hawley, my long-time People Officer at Return Path and Bolster, is the principal author and she is the one who has the experience, credibility, and expertise to share something of value with others in the People function. This material was also read and edited by additional CPOs we know.

One caveat. Although this book is being written by Cathy and me, it is not meant to be the Return Path story. We each have 20–30 years of experience working at multiple companies of different sizes and at different stages and in different sectors on which we are drawing. It's also not the story of Bolster, the new company that a number of us started during the pandemic in 2020. The book is based on our experience mostly in U.S.-based tech or tech-enabled services businesses, and more from the perspective of B2B than B2C, though inclusive of both. A few notes on language. We realize that not every leadership role in a startup is actually a "C"-level role. Sometimes the most senior person running a functional department is an SVP, a VP, a "head of," or even a Director or Manager. But Startup Functional Leader is a lousy title for a book. Regardless of title, we wrote with the most senior person responsible for the People function in mind. Another point on terminology is that we use the words startup and scaleup in the book without precise revenue-based or employee-count-based definitions, but you should assume that startups are smaller companies, whereas scaleups are ones that have already reached some meaningful level of critical mass. We also use terms like "executive team," "leadership team," "C-suite" and "executive committee" interchangeably to refer to a company's senior-most group of leaders. Finally, we frequently refer to the concept of an "operating system." I talked about this at length in my earlier book, *Startup CEO,* but basically, it means––whether for a person, a team, or a company––the collection of meeting and communication routines and operating practices that form the cadence of a team's work.

Although the book is focused on the CPO role, there are insights for others in an organization. So, if you're a CEO, you could gain some additional insight into why something is not working in your People organization––and understand how and what to change to create success in your People team. I also have a "CEO-to-CEO Advice" section where I share my thoughts on what "great" looks like for the CPO, signs that your CPO isn't scaling, and how I engage with the CPO. I believe (and hope!) that CEOs, Board members, and investors can quickly get an overview and understanding of the CPO function by reading the "CEO-to-CEO Advice" chapter.

If you are a CPO or aspiring to become one, I hope this book speaks to you and inspires you in some way––that it's a playbook for something meaningful to you. If you're a CEO, maybe it will help you figure out who to hire or how to more effectively manage your CPO by telling you what "great" looks like for a CPO. If you're already a CPO in a startup, maybe it will help you focus on some aspect of your role you hadn't thought about yet. If you're an aspiring leader, maybe it will give you some insight into the kinds of steps you need to take in order to grow your career. Whichever persona you are, on behalf of me and Cathy, we hope you gain some insight, and we thank you for reading *Startup CPO: A Field Guide to Scaling up Your Company's HR/People Function.*

I. WELCOME TO THE EXECUTIVE TEAM

Matt Blumberg

1

The Nature of a CXO's Role

I was struck by something as I read over the nearly complete manuscript of *Startup CXO* for the first time: each CXO believes that their part of the business is the most important part. And they make a compelling set of arguments:

Shawn: If you don't have a good product, you don't have a business.

Anita: If you don't have revenues, you don't have a business.

Ken: If you don't develop the ecosystem, you don't have a business.

Nick: If you don't generate market opportunities, you don't have a business.

George: If you don't create exceptional customer experiences, you don't have a business.

Cathy: If you don't recruit, train, and develop the right people, you don't have a business.

Jack: If you don't have the cash, you don't have a business.

Dennis: If you don't bake privacy in at the beginning, you don't have a business.

We had a debate years ago at a Return Path Board meeting as to whether we were a sales-driven business or a product-driven business—and more important, whether we should be one or the other.

Two of our Board members, both of whom I respect tremendously, were anchoring the different points of view, Scott Petry, on the product side, talking about how successful Apple was at getting customers to camp out overnight to be the first ones to buy the newest iThing; and Greg Sands, on the sales side, talking about how successful Oracle was at getting product into the hands of customers. I took a devil's advocate point of view in the conversation, true to our operating philosophy at Return Path, which was that HR/People was the most important function because we were a people-driven business.

So, who is right? Are the best companies sales-driven, product-driven, people-driven, or something else? Which of the CXO's functions is the most important? My answer is—they all are important, just in different ways, at different times, and in different combinations. While it's the CEO's job to balance the functions out—to figure out which lever to pull at which time, it's the CXO's job to be at the ready when their lever is pulled. And that gets to the important question of what the nature of a CXO role is, and why those roles can be tricky. CXOs have three principal jobs that they must keep in balance at all times, although there is a clear priority in my mind of the three jobs.

CXOs are first and foremost members of the company's Executive Team. They must, must, must put that team, understanding of the different functions, and the relationships on it at the top of their agenda. They shouldn't show up on the team only advocating for their own team. CEOs must insist on that behavior and mentality. Without it, a company simply can't function sustainably. This concept is one that we have always called the First Team concept, and it's articulated very eloquently by Patrick Lencioni in a number of his books, particularly in *The Five Dysfunctions of a Team* and *The Advantage.* As members of the Executive Team, all CXOs are accountable to each other for the success of the business as a whole and must partner with each other to achieve that success.

CXOs are also the head of their respective functional departments. They must carry the flag of their team and wave it proudly throughout the organization, especially when working with their teams. They are the functional role model, the functional mentor, and the functional decision-maker for the people on their functional team. To be an effective leader, they must be The Quintessential X (sales professional, engineer, marketer, etc.).

Finally, CXOs are company leaders. They are role models for company values. They should always be on alert for things that are going well or going poorly around them. Things that need attention or recognition. Situations that need calming down. Guests who are sitting unattended in the office lobby. Delivery people who need a check signed and who need to be tipped. Putting the new bottle of water onto the water cooler. You get the idea. Company leaders have the actual and moral authority to step outside of their departments and handle things as they need to be handled, regardless of which employees are involved.

2

Scaling a CPO

Congratulations, you just got promoted from Director of People to CPO! You're now in charge of a whole functional department, you now report to the CEO, you're now on the Executive Committee. You have a whole bunch of direct reports that either represent the team you used to lead or yesterday were your peers and you have now reached the pinnacle of your career in the People organization. The only other ways to grow your career vertically are to lead your function at a larger and larger company, or to become a CEO. Wow!

That feeling of euphoria is wonderful. I remember having it when I worked at MovieFone and became the head of marketing and product management instead of just the "Internet guy." It definitely led to a nice celebratory night out in Manhattan with friends.

But then, the reality set in the next morning. Uh oh. I've never done this job before. Maybe I know how to do 25% of it. I'm only 26 years old. Is anyone going to respect me? I have so much to learn. Can I fake it? How on earth did I find myself here? This phenomenon is called the Imposter Syndrome, and it's totally normal. In fact, if you grow your career quickly, it would be weird not to have at least a touch of it.

The good news is, you're not the first person to be promoted to an executive role for the first time (and of course you're not the last, either). Every single executive, at any company, had their first executive role at some point. While there's some credence to the expression "fake it till you make it," there's a more methodical approach you can take to scaling yourself as a CPO—or if you're the CEO, to helping your new CPO scale. Think of the journey in three steps that can be taken in any order.

First, master the tactics. You need to understand all of the things that happen in your department. Some, you will know well because they're the ones you've done over time. Some you won't know at all. Make sure you do a complete inventory of the functional competencies for your role and all the roles reporting to you. Depending on how organized your company is with job descriptions and what's often known as a RACI (responsible-accountable-consulted-informed) analysis, this may be as easy as pulling something off the shelf and having a series of meetings with the people on your team to walk you through what they do. If your company isn't that organized, you may want to take the opportunity to proactively build that kind of functional competency/RACI list for every-thing in your team. That is no small exercise, but it's one that will pay back massive dividends. As one of my long-time colleagues, Anita Absey, says, "What gets measured gets managed." I'd add to that: if you don't know something even exists, you can't begin to measure it, let alone manage it!

Second, form your strategic approach. Every single function in a com-pany has tactical and transactional elements to it—and every single function can be ONLY tactical if you let it. That's the lowest common denominator. HR can be about benefits and payroll. Sales can be about pipeline management and closing deals. Marketing can be about blog posts and SEO. A transactional focus is especially true of corporate functions like HR and Finance, but it's true of all functions. But just as every function has its tactical elements that must be attended to, every function CAN be strategic. As you settle into your new role, and as you grow into the role of senior executive and learn the First Team lesson of putting the needs of the business before the needs of your department, you will be able to start thinking more holistically about the business and how your department fits into it, so when your CEO pulls the lever that indicates they need your team to step up and lead, to be strategic on some topic, you are ready. What does it mean to be strategic vs. tactical? It's the difference between eating what's on your plate and planning out next week's menu. What are the ways in which the People organization can produce competitive differentiation for the business? What are the frameworks that will guide your decision-making about resource allocation or prioritization? How can you best support the other departments in the company? Those are the kinds of things you need to master in step 2. As my colleague Dave Wilby once said about one of the teams he was managing, "We have to figure out how to be the nose, not the tail."

Finally, look around the corner to see what's next for you and for your team. Senior executives constantly need to be toggling between different execution and planning horizons. You need to make your goals this quarter, and to make them, you have to hit daily or weekly activity metrics and milestones. But what about next quarter? Or next year? Or what happens if your company doubles in size in the next six months and is set to double again? Start by revisiting that functional competency/RACI list from step 1 and stress-test every element of it. Ask yourself, What must be true of this line item when the company is twice its current size? While you have to develop and scale as a leader—with all that goes into that in terms of soft skills—the only way to scale yourself as a CPO is to understand what great looks like for your role at the next stage of the company's life, and make sure you don't get there after your company needs you to.

All three of these steps—mastering the tactics of your department, forming your strategic approach, and understanding what's next—are things you may be able to do on your own to a point. That said, they will all go more quickly and with a higher probability of success if you engage your CEO, your Head of HR, members of your Board, or outside mentors or coaches to assist you on your journey.

II. CHIEF PEOPLE OFFICER

Cathy Hawley and Matt Blumberg

Bolster Network

Chief People Officer

Cathy Hawley

Human Resources has evolved from transactional, compliance focused administrative work to more strategic, proactive work that touches all aspects of the business. The work is much more rewarding and impactful now. This section focuses on the "new HR" which I'll call "People," and also focuses on a particular framing for People leaders who want to help a CEO and leadership team create a people-centric, values-driven, learning organization and culture that optimizes the contribution and experience of employees and their impact to the company. Trust me, as someone who has experienced traditional HR and also worked with CEOs who are *only* business- and not people-focused, strategically driving a people-focused company is much more rewarding and impactful. If your founder/CEO has interest in building a values-driven company, you'll find this book relevant to your success. I've been lucky to work with Matt at both Return Path and at Bolster, and his mentorship and guidance helped me be more impactful in my People roles, and also expand my skillset to set me up for a role outside the People function. At Bolster, I've held a variety of different roles, probably best described as COO for the first 4 years, in preparation for succession into the CEO role in June 2024.

I started my career in a very traditional HR role as the HR Manager at a 100-person truck stop. I did everything you'd expect in that role including hiring, processing payroll, writing an employee manual, dealing with workers' compensation claims ... if it was remotely connected to compliance, I did it. The truck stop was hierarchical, had traditional gender roles, and no one was consulted on any decision since the CEO made all the decisions himself. Although I knew I couldn't thrive there in the long term, I did learn everything about transactional HR that they don't teach you in college, like how to actually run payroll, negotiate benefits, manage difficult employee situations, and manage risk. My role was to focus on the company first, by making sure that we mitigated risk and reduced costs. Many HR people started their careers in similar environments, and, without the benefit of a more open-minded CEO or company, they become the HR Directors of comic strips.

Luckily, my career shifted after that and I later had the opportunity to work with technology companies whose cultures were focused on people––on trusting that you've hired adults who don't need "managing," and focused on providing development opportunities for people. At these companies my role was to focus on both the business and on people, and help us make good business decisions that were best for people.

Both business-first and people-centric/inclusive companies exist today. If you're an early-stage startup, and have a CEO who cares deeply about people, help them create a people-centric/inclusive environment. Building a sustainable company that people love to work for will drive engagement and business results. When someone feels included, and can bring their whole self to work, when they don't have to worry about being judged for having different opinions or ways of working, they do better work. They can focus on the task at hand rather than worrying about what people think, or whether they will be heard if they have an opinion.

At Return Path, we didn't explicitly start with building an inclusive culture. Luckily, the founders and early team members did have a bias toward inclusion and they built a lot of practices and processes that led toward an inclusive environment. At Bolster, we are intentionally building inclusion into our strategy and culture (and in our case, it's related to our actual product offering, too). You'll see people-centric and inclusive practices throughout this book that are different from those you've seen at many companies and you'll see how they lead to a more inclusive environment. It's not easy to be inclusive without the support of your CEO since you'll continually have to educate and influence leaders and employees to embrace a different way of working. Having your CEO embrace and lead that education and influence with you is powerful. In my experience, there are more CEOs right now who want to build an inclusive culture than there are HR leaders who have the skills and experience to do this, so the quicker you can embrace the mindset and build the skills required, the more impact you can make at your company and in the world!

Payroll, benefits, and people operations are, of course, urgent in a startup. I'll touch on those later in Chapter 18. These are table stakes and don't highly differentiate you, so I'll start with what I think is your most important role: building an inclusive culture.

As Chief People Officer, you will have far more tasks to complete than time available to you and I have highlighted the critical things needed to scale: articulating your values, building diversity, equity, and inclusion into your foundation, building your team, setting up structures and practices that lead to the culture you desire, leadership development, recruiting, people operations, onboarding, talent management, organizational design, and team development. Each chapter provides ideas, tools, and issues for the startup and scaleup phases so you can both learn about your current situation and also see what's on the horizon. I realize that the journey from startup to scaleup is not linear and there are times when you need to reduce headcount and I have a chapter on best practices for doing that (Chapter 15).

Values and Culture

Driving alignment on values and culture will guide you in nearly everything you do. Your values help you find and hire the right people, reward and recognize people and behaviors, influence your organizational structure and operating system, and help you make decisions. Your values also shape the things you don't want to do, or shouldn't do: they prevent you from hiring people who don't fit your company, they guide you on the markets you'd like to enter, or ones you don't want to enter, and they frame how you select vendors and customers. Your values also influence the culture that you build.

Culture is the sum of the everyday behaviors of employees—how work gets done, how people interact with each other, and how they exemplify the values. For example, if leadership team members make every decision themselves without including others, you'll soon find that the culture of the company is one in which everyone waits for a leader to make a decision before they take action.

You may run into a CEO who just wants to build a business and isn't interested in the culture. They may believe that business takes priority over culture, that culture is just "soft stuff," or that it doesn't add value. There's a quote attributed to Peter Drucker that "culture eats strategy for breakfast"; as Chief People Officer, it's important for you to help people understand the importance of culture to *support* the business strategy. I don't advocate for culture *over* strategy. It's just that many executives focus *only* on strategy, and you can help them add culture to their perspectives. If you're in this situation, you can help paint the picture of what the company will look like if you aren't focused on culture and values from the very start. You are going to have a culture, and the options are to build it intentionally or let it happen by chance!

Every person you hire at an early stage has an outsized impact on the culture. If their values don't match those of the CEO or executive team, they won't be successful in the organization, or they will build a toxic subculture that is hard to dismantle. Until they leave the company, there will be tension and unproductive conflict which wastes time, resources, and impacts productivity and engagement. For example, suppose you have a CEO who values transparency and direct conversations and you hire a leader who is more political and is not transparent with their colleagues. That individual is unlikely to be successful, and the reverse is true as well.

Being able to hone in on the values and culture your team wants is an iterative process, and the starting point will differ depending on how strong a vision the CEO/founders/leadership team have about culture. The number of people involved in the initial process can make a difference, too. If you have three people, you can become aligned more quickly than if you have a dozen people. To get things going, have conversations with a small group of people, just the CEO and founders or, if the team is small, the full leadership team. Start with a conversation about what matters to the stakeholders: What do they care most about and what's the best culture they can envision? Or, you can start by asking what legacy the CEO/founders would like to see the company have. Here are a few topics you can ask about:

- How do you think about hierarchy and decision making? Do decisions need to be made at the top, or do you want people to feel empowered to make decisions themselves?

- What is the level of transparency that you want? Do you hold this as a value? Would you rather be fully transparent about everything, or operate on a "need-to-know" basis?

- Will you embrace a remote culture, or do you want people to work in the office? (This topic is especially important right now, as we manage through the global pandemic. It's an opportunity for companies to rethink their priorities and explore whether a remote culture works for them.)

- How important is diversity to you? If important, what does it mean to you?

- How do you feel about corporate social responsibility? As a start-up, how much effort do you want to focus on this?

- How innovative do you want or need to be?

- Do you value speed over quality?

- What's your financial model? Will you reinvest any profits in growth? What responsibility do you feel for sharing profits with employees?

- Do you value a work hard/play hard model or do you want to focus on more of a work-life balance?

- Do you have a preference for building everything in-house, or are you willing to partner or outsource?

Your role as Chief People Officer is to help continue that conversation, to facilitate it so that alternative voices are heard, until you have enough content to articulate that culture. Once you're comfortable (as a team) on the culture, shift your focus to values. Look online to find lists of company values—either through articles or looking at different companies' websites and pull together a starting list of values for the team to explore. The list should be broad and encompass some of the diverging viewpoints you heard. You'll want to have another conversation with the CEO/founders/leadership team about values. Your aim in this conversation is to narrow down the values list to the most important three to seven values.

Getting alignment on culture and values is the best use of your time as a startup Chief People Officer and the results will carry the company far, since the culture and values impact every facet of how you work together and how you approach and solve problems. Your company's values need to be ingrained within the people in your company and it's something that you, as Chief People Officer, will measure, evaluate, champion, and help course-correct as your company scales.

As you grow, you'll want to build deep skills in the company on how to talk about your values and tell stories that demonstrate your values in action. This helps to make values part of your company's DNA and when you grow, the values will grow with you. While people may have an intellectual understanding of values, they'll also need to be able to see them in action concretely, and you'll have to help them recognize and reward values-based behaviors. At Return Path, we built values into every people practice: we interviewed people on values alignment, we had story-telling sessions during onboarding, all our rewards were based on a value, we highlighted people who embodied the values, and we evaluated values-based behavior in promotions and performance.

You'll also periodically evaluate whether the stated values still accurately reflect the actual and desired behaviors. Generally, values don't change over time but they might if you've experienced a change in leadership or if you realize that you missed or misstated some values at the beginning. It's not uncommon for the leadership team to refine the values over time, to help them be more clearly understood by employees. This is especially important if you're growing very fast, if you have remote workers, or if you're geographically dispersed.

At Return Path, about 10 years after our founding (in 2008), we experienced a large growth spurt, including international growth. We weren't sure if the mission and values we started with reflected who we had become. We ran a company-wide values exercise to better understand what was most important to employees. Everyone at the company joined one of a series of small-group brainstorming sessions where we discussed current values and mission and recommended changes. Matt took the results and recommendations from all those sessions and crafted our revised values framework. It turned out that the revised values weren't too different but were reframed in a way that was easier for people to understand.

You can find many examples of values on company websites; here are the final values from Return Path; you can see that Matt had some fun with the acronym!

Our Path to Going **A**bove and **B**eyond the **C**all of **D**uty for **E**veryone. We are...

Owners
Unconventional
Results Oriented
People First
Agile
Transparent
Helpful
Appreciative
Business Focused
Collaborative
Data Driven
Equity in Opportunity

A few other companies that have impactful values include, Sendgrid (hungry, happy, honest, humble), Twilio (centered around how we act, how we make decisions, how we win), and Moz (transparent, authentic, generous, fun empathetic, exceptional).

At Bolster, we wanted to make sure that our values were very clear and easily remembered, and also raised the bar. Some values that we articulated at Return Path are just table stakes for us here, so we were diligent about articulating values that are really clear and explicit. We also distinguished between values (rarely changing) and operating principles (dependent on stage). Our values are:

- Always Have Heart: We treat everyone with respect and value the unique individuality of our employees, members, and clients. We are helpful and thankful, inclusive, and assume positive intent.

- Be Transparent: We help others understand our thought process; show our data, and facilitate honest and open feedback.

- Continuous Growth: We are intellectually curious, and this helps us to grow. We strive to be and to develop high-performing individuals, teams, company, members, and clients.

- Do the Right Thing: We always err on the side of high integrity and putting company, members, and clients above self, even when that is difficult.

The work that you do as Chief People Officer on your company values and your culture will be some of the most impactful work you do. You'll need to revisit the conversation over time to make sure the values and culture are still relevant as you grow. Values generally don't change over time, but your culture may. Either way, you'll have to be intentional about revisiting conversations on culture and values.

What I Look for in a Chief People Officer

My dream HR and People leader embodies a unique blend of characteristics, skills, and experiences. Just like the CFO, this startup leader needs to be honest, ethical, and have strong character. Trust is the foundation for this role. Building on this foundation, I am then looking for the right mix of tactical and strategic HR experience. On the tactical or transactional side, the leader needs to be proficient in getting key systems and processes running smoothly—payroll, compensation, benefits plan, performance review process, performance improvement plans (when needed), employee handbook, employee onboarding, etc.. Stretching further, I am looking for this leader to build HR into a strategic function, not just a transactional function. First step is helping the CEO develop core values and a culture framework. And most importantly, working to reinforce these values through actions, behavior modeling, and excellent company communication. Next up is recruiting with urgency, discipline, and high standards of excellence. Is anything more important than attracting the best talent possible and helping them achieve their full potential? Building diverse teams and an inclusive culture has never been more important. Most of all, I am looking for the startup Head of HR to be an amazing business partner to the CEO, to the leadership team, and to the company at large. This person needs to take care of small problems, bring positive energy, surface new opportunities, keep a pulse on the organization, and build trusting relationships. All these tasks are a critical part of the charter. In many ways, the HR and People leader is the glue that brings every functional group together. And cross-functional collaboration is imperative to company success. As an investor and Board member, I sleep better at night knowing that our portfolio company has a star HR and People leader who is extraordinarily trustworthy and reliable and will make the CEO, team, and company better every day. **Scott Dorsey,** *Managing Partner, High Alpha*

5

Diversity, Equity, and Inclusion (DE&I)

We noted earlier that building an inclusive culture will reap many rewards in the long term. In every aspect of the People function you can build practices to interrupt unconscious bias and create a more inclusive workplace. Intentionally building DE&I into the foundation of your organization is much more impactful than trying to retro-fit it later. We use the term "DE&I" rather than just diversity or inclusion, because it's not enough to bring in diverse talent to make sure that your organization is representative of your location. If you don't compensate people equitably, then you won't retain or engage your newly diverse workforce. If the people you hire don't feel included, they can't have the psychological safety that is required to be the best team member they can be. It's a lot of work to uncover and interrupt our cultural biases, but it's critical for a number of reasons:

- It's the right thing to do.

- There's a business case for diversity, demonstrating that more diverse Boards and leadership teams have higher valuations and growth, and diverse teams are more innovative.

- Building a just and equitable company where people have access to opportunities is becoming more expected by the people you want to hire. It is the new standard for being a great place to work.

- DE&I won't just happen on its own. Even with the best intentions, there is systemic and individual bias. To overcome these, you must be intentional about adapting traditional methods of sourcing, recruiting, compensation, promotions, and performance management. You need to counter the biases in our systems and help people understand how to proactively engage in inclusive behaviors.

If you don't start out with DE&I as the core cultural value at your company, what can you do, as Chief People Officer, to get there quickly? One tactic we found helpful at Return Path was to partner with an organization that was an expert in shifting to a DE&I-focus. We partnered with the National Center for Women in Information Technology (NCWIT), which is where we learned a lot about DE&I (and not just about women in technology!). Our partners at NCWIT, and especially Jill Reckie, helped us to think about DE&I strategically and comprehensively. Leveraging our learning and partnership with NCWIT, we built an internal DE&I team that was incredibly impactful. A senior People team member led the overall initiative which included volunteers from across the organization split into work groups, focused on different parts of the employee lifecycle. In many cases, the People team functional lead participated with the work group so they could implement the programmatic recommendations. Even with strong systems set up, we always looked for ways that unconscious bias was filtering in. Given that we all have our own personal experience and journey and it's hard to deeply understand another person's journey through our own personal lens, it was really important to include diverse voices and perspectives in these work groups.

See www.startuprev.com for a chart showing our work groups and examples of the work completed in each.

6

Building Your Team

As a startup you'll need to be scrappy and hire people who also can wear multiple hats. Your first hire should be someone whose skills complement yours, and they also need to understand that startups don't have processes and procedures in place that can be followed or modified. There is more uncertainty and things change rapidly, even with the best planning. And your first hire needs to understand that the People role is every bit as entrepreneurial as any other role. While you'll create a strategic People plan that aligns with the company's strategic plan and covers recruiting, organizational design and development, and operations, your first hire must be comfortable shifting between roles, embracing change and uncertainty, and have values alignment with the company. Ideally, you can provide a pathway for growth and opportunities to expand their skills, allowing this individual to grow with the organization and be your right-hand person as the company moves from startup to scaleup.

As the organization grows, you'll need to continually evaluate whether you are sufficiently staffed for the next stage of growth, and able to achieve your strategic plan. I recommend that your team's growth plan be tied to the growth in the number of people in your company and not revenues. In an established company with a repeatable revenue stream, it's easier to plan for people growth, but in a startup the need for people usually outstrips revenues. If you wait to hit revenue milestones, you'll find that you are severely understaffed and when you do hire people, they will spend their time catching up on things left undone rather than being focused on growth. You'll also need to hire people who can be scrappy and not be perfectionists. I hired a really smart woman once who cared a lot about her job, but didn't move quickly and needed everything very orderly before she could switch tasks. She spent days putting all our employee files into folders that required two-hole punches in the top of each page, and a separate tab for each type of paperwork, which then also meant a lot of time per file setup. That type of heavy organization doesn't work in a startup, even though her responsibilities included ensuring that we had the right paperwork for each employee.

After your first hire, you should think about scaling your team, and building for scope and breadth by hiring specialty roles. Your second hire is just as critical as the first hire and I recommend that you consider hiring someone from inside the company, someone who understands the business and demonstrates interest in people—maybe someone who connects with others at the company, welcomes new people, and offers to help them understand the company. This person may never have thought about a People Operations role and most likely is not trained for it. That's OK! You will be better served at this stage of growth providing your own training on the technical skills.

Early on at Return Path, we promoted our office manager, Amanda McDermott, to run payroll and benefits. Her predecessor stayed at the company in another role, so was able to provide training and support, and Amanda also completed some online courses to learn more. She had the right customer-focused mindset and process orientation, and she also knew the employees and the business. Learning payroll was easy for her and she continued to grow in the People Operations role as the company grew. If you're not ready yet to promote from within, keep that in mind for when you become larger. I've done it both ways: hiring a traditional HR person and shifting them to a people-focused role, and hiring a people person and training them on technical skills. I was more successful with the latter, as I didn't have to help people "unlearn" their old habits of being more compliance focused. If you've been creative about your People practices, I would recommend this approach.

As a startup with a small team, you'll be managing many roles and responsibilities. As you grow, these roles will need to be filled by others, including People Business Partner, Talent Acquisition/Recruiting, People Operations, and later Onboarding and Leadership Development. You'll generally maintain your role of building an intentional culture, building values into your DNA, coaching the executive team, and building and growing your team. The following roles are critical for success.

Critical Roles

There's one caution here for companies that are experiencing a lot of growth: it's easy for any team in your company, including People Operations, to become so maniacally focused on their part of the business that they become insular and siloed. That sets the stage for subcultures to emerge. You'll need to ensure that the People team has a really strong operating system to ensure they are focusing on the most important and impactful work, that the team collaborates effectively with each other and the rest of the company, and that all team members keep each other informed.

As your team grows and develops, you'll want leaders for each of the different functional areas. If you're growing rapidly it's easy to justify bringing in a senior manager to work with a functional area, and if you're relatively small, it's easy to justify not hiring a manager. But what if you're stuck in the middle? Too small to hire someone but too big to be without managers? One solution to that problem is to designate a leader for each functional area and keep everyone reporting to you—the leader and everyone on the functional team. While it can be a little confusing at times, having every function explicitly owned by someone, even if one person covers more than one function. Be explicit about ownership, so you don't forget important parts of your strategic roadmap.

If you're scaling the People team, the logical first managers will be in People Operations and Organizational Development and you will have systems and people in place for the entire organization. Once you've designated leaders for those two functional areas, make sure that your operating system is updated to include a leadership meeting so leaders can stay aligned on strategy, and guide their teams effectively. Of course, you'll want to continue to have full team meetings as well, so that all functional team members still have relationships and visibility into everything happening on the team and in the business. You'll also want to ensure that you invest time every quarter on team development and deepening skills and emotional intelligence on your team. Your team members need to embody the values of the organization and be role models in their behavior. Keep in mind too that it's really common for a People team to care so much about others in the organization that they neglect themselves. As the Chief People Officer, you need to be aware of this tendency and know your team well enough that you can spot when people are too emotionally invested in the goings on of a company. While you can't completely eliminate this tendency, you can identify it quickly and take steps to minimize the impact. If you have a strong operating system that includes regular leadership and team development, one-to-ones with members of your team, and a level of trust where people can admit that they are struggling, you can help your team stay focused and balanced.

As you continue to grow, the sub-functions may be ready for their own leaders or managers but there's a tradeoff in scaling by creating subgroups with managers and that is usually less speed and nimbleness. I try to keep the hierarchy as light as possible and prefer to create team leader roles instead of manager roles. I also use the same employee/manager/organizational structure guidelines for the People Operations team that we use in other parts of the organization. That way you have structural alignment company-wide and that makes promotions, compensation, and career pathing similar across the whole company.

A powerful way to extend your reach and share responsibility for cultural stewardship is to get a network of volunteers from other teams at the company to drive different people-related programs. Make it a requirement for each employee to "give back" to the community. At Return Path, we had volunteers who ran social events, community service programs, our well-being program, and our diversity, equity, and inclusion programs. The People Team managed the programs globally, gave direction, guidance, and budget for local committees.

If you are creating, or already have, a values-driven company, the People team is critical to the success for the business. We would even argue (although our colleagues might disagree!) that the People team are the true drivers of a company and impact both top-line growth and productivity. Values and culture impact hiring, turnover, engagement, morale, and productivity. There's a measurable effect of culture and values on innovation.

7

Organizational Design and Operating Systems

B e intentional about your organizational design from the beginning, and evaluate it periodically to ensure that your design principles still align with your company values and stage of growth. Use the data you collect from exit interviews, turnover, employee surveys, and employee conversations to determine if the design and principles are still relevant.

Your initial design work will be with the CEO, and will also engage the leadership team. Your work on organizational design is not theoretical, or something that stands alone. Just the opposite! It goes hand-in-hand with culture and values conversations. Your organizational design will never be perfect and will always have tradeoffs to consider. There's a saying that you should "never let perfect be the enemy of good" and that's the case with organizational design. As long as your design aligns with your culture and values, it ought to serve its purpose, which is to help people be as productive and engaged as possible and to ensure that there is the right flow of communication between people and teams.

There are a few things to build in from the beginning, including practices around manager span of control, manager role, cross-functional teams, and how you think about hierarchy. People have preconceived notions about all aspects of organizations, and having conversations with the leadership team to help them think about the implications of organizational design principles is critical. It's really easy to grow too hierarchical where managers have small spans of control or if you hire managers who have a "command and control" style. You can help leaders get creative about career development when a team isn't big enough for a leader, and employees want to take on leadership roles. Employees in this situation can expand their role by managing workflow, team operating systems, or projects, without becoming the team manager.

In the beginning, you may not have executive leaders for all the different functional areas, so some executives will lead functions that are new to them. You may have a COO who is also leading Sales, or a CFO leading Technology. Help ensure that leaders who are responsible for several functional areas hire functional experts or get strong mentorship in the areas where they aren't as knowledgeable.

It's best to evaluate organizational structure every six to twelve months for effectiveness, and to make small adjustments, or do a full redesign and restructure if absolutely necessary. Often as you grow, you realize that you've prioritized role function over product/division, and you may need to swing the pendulum the other direction. While every organization has different needs, many organizations are moving toward flatter, more networked, team-based structures. These structures need even more clear leadership and operating systems to be most effective.

Being Transparent About Changes

At DoubleClick, my division managed global services for all product lines. Each product line would separately modify their investment in services based on the success of their products. When the key executive and I started in the division, small regular layoffs were standard. The Product line would reduce their investment, and then the Services organization would reduce their staff. This resulted in a lack of engagement and productivity, as people were constantly wondering if they were going to be next to go. In addition, changes were made without any notice. One day, you'd be working alongside a colleague; the next day their desk would be cleared out. I worked with the new executive to understand the impact of these reactive changes, and we agreed on a new process. We created strong career pathing so people could move between roles and product service areas, and we also created a planning process for each product area to follow, so we were able to predict need and manage our staffing appropriately. At one stage, we decided on a large-scale change in roles, and proposed a consultation process that included transparency and engagement of employees. We were modifying over 100 roles, and this would result in a reduction of 20% overall. Within a week, we communicated the changes, asked people their preferences, assessed skills, and made all the role-change decisions. Some people voluntarily left the organization and others took on new roles. There was some risk in this approach, and many of our internal clients were worried about losing their best service people. The result of the transparency and employee input was that we retained everyone critical to the organization, and people were more highly engaged than before the reorganization. **Cathy Hawley,** *CEO,* ***Bolster***

At Return Path, we made changes to the organizational structure periodically. At one point, we realized that one of our new product areas wasn't getting the right level of focus from the different functions. It was a new product and wasn't driving a lot of revenue, and when each functional team prioritized their work, this new product was last on the priority list. We moved the product into its own cross-functional team that was managed separately from all the other functional teams to ensure we created the right focus within the company. Another time, we knew one area of the business needed to be divested, so we moved all our teams into cross-functional business units, which made the sale much cleaner from both a balance-sheet and people perspective.

When you change your organizational structure, there will be a lot of questions from employees and some anxiety on what those changes mean for them. To effectively lead an organizational redesign, you'll need to make sure you follow your company values and principles as closely as possible, to speed up the transition, because when you make decisions that impact people's role, manager or compensation, every moment employees spend thinking about the change is a moment when they are not being productive. Be as inclusive as possible in the decision-making process and people will embrace change more readily. Common thinking is that the primary role of a manager/leader is to make decisions *about* people. That common thinking is limiting and defines the "command and control" model of leadership. If at all possible, it is more effective to make decisions *with* people, to be inclusive and collaborative. An inclusive approach takes longer and can be more difficult and it is also much more effective, more motivating, and leads to better results in the long run. People are more engaged, the more they are able to co-create their environment and success measures. The leader's role can be to ensure that everyone is aligned and moving in the same direction.

Alongside the organizational design, you'll want to work with the CEO and leadership team to create a company-wide operating system. By "operating system," I don't mean a bureaucratic structure that serves to control people or burden them with reporting requirements just so senior leadership can be informed. I mean a transparent process that shows how often, where, and when your team will meet, how they will determine and prioritize their work, how they will communicate and connect with other teams at the company, and how they will hold each other accountable for results. A strong operating system that changes as the business changes helps ensure that all teams are aligned and working toward the same goals, and holding each other accountable for results.

One of the most impactful changes we managed at Return Path was a company-wide agile transformation project. For years we used agile methodologies in our engineering department, and in December 2013, the week before my sabbatical, Matt challenged us to shift the entire company to agile practices by June 2014. When I returned in mid-January, a team of four of us from the People and Program Management teams ran this project (along with our normal roles!). This was one of my favorite and most impactful cross-functional teams so I'll call out my team: Mike Mills, Caroline Pearl, and Jane Ritter, with support from Dan Corbin. By June 2014, we had completed pilots with 12 teams, developed a framework for five team types to leverage agile practices, and trained 50 facilitators in how to effect change in their team's operating practices. In addition to the individual team changes, we modified the entire company operating system to leverage agile practices. We increased productivity by 13% in one year; we measured this by looking at a number of different metrics, the most relevant to other organizations being revenue per person.

Along with a company-wide operating system, help to build your leadership team operating system. When you are small, this may be as simple as a tactical leadership team meeting twice a week, a strategic meeting once a week, and a company-wide meeting once a week for everyone to share progress on goals and hold each other accountable. Patrick Lencioni's book, *Death by Meeting*, is a good resource to help you think through the different types of team meetings and how to run them.

You can also help establish these norms across the company. I recommend helping teams leverage agile practices: build a strategic roadmap, engage stakeholders in your work, align on prioritization, remove roadblocks in real time, collaborate on big projects, and keep a backlog so you aren't just responsive to every request that comes to you. It's really easy to fall into the trap of working on the most urgent rather than the most important. There are always fires to put out and having a strategic roadmap and a good operating system is critical for success.

Your operating system is not fixed in place for all time; you'll need to evaluate it periodically, and test to see whether it still serves its purpose, and redesign as appropriate. As you grow and change, your operating systems will need to be updated for your new organization structure. At the startup stage you may be able to pull everyone into one room for an informal company update. But when you grow beyond the one-room company stage, you'll want to partner with your marketing/corporate communications team to develop more robust communication practices to ensure alignment.

At Return Path, we had an operating system that changed every year, except for the annual "un-Roadshow." The un-Roadshow was a company-wide kickoff to help everyone understand the final output of the annual strategic planning. Each team contributed to the plan, and no teams had seen the full and final plan. The un-Roadshow always included in-person time with the full leadership team for people to ask questions and have unscripted dialog to ensure they fully understood how their roles fit into the strategic plans for the year. The format was changed every year to keep the programming as unique and engaging as possible. The rest of the year included quarterly planning and retrospective meetings with all team leaders, distribution to all employees of the Board Book, and all hands meetings to discuss progress against goals. We followed up with roundtable discussions with leadership team members. It's a lot of work to maintain a strong operating system, and requires partnership with the CEO. It may not be your responsibility, but you'll definitely play a role in its creation and maintenance. See www.startuprev.com for the final company-wide operating system at Return Path.

8

Team Development

Almost all companies require collaboration within the team to get work done. Even if cross-functional collaboration isn't required for each person's primary responsibilities, teams still need to collaborate on effective practices and processes to achieve their shared goals. Many companies only focus on team development at the leadership team level, and then on team "building" for other teams. All teams benefit from having support and intention around how they operate and interact. Skills built around team development for the core team also help each individual be a better team member when they work cross-functionally.

At startup level the most important team is the leadership team, as they impact the entire company. It's absolutely critical that the leadership team build a high level of trust and the ability to have productive conflict. There's always going to be conflict; it's unavoidable. But it doesn't have to be debilitating or result in damaged relationships. If there are high levels of trust, conflict can be extremely helpful to the team. There are many tools and assessments you can use to help with team diagnostics, and the most impactful, and simple, tool we've used is Patrick Lencioni's book, *The Five Dysfunctions of a Team*. (Lencioni's book, *The Advantage*, combines his thinking in both the prior books mentioned (*Death by Meeting* and *The Five Dysfunctions of a Team*), as well as introducing an annual planning framework that we adopted and modified at Return

Path with great success). Do yourself and your company a favor and take the 5-minute assessment every quarter, evaluate the results as a team, and agree to the development you need to make the team successful. The type of development the team requires depends on the results of the survey: if you score low on trust, work to deepen relationships. If you score low on conflict, understand the underlying reasons, and then offer coaching or development on conflict. Having a highly functioning leadership team sets the stage for having a highly functioning organization. Without that, it's very difficult to keep teams aligned and working together effectively.

In addition to building an effective leadership team, you may also facilitate strategy development and planning discussions or offsites. Some of the most impactful work you do will be to help your leadership team have deep conversations on business strategy. Strategy development discussions are not just straightforward conversations and it's crucial to build an agenda that helps drive toward your goals. It's often helpful to partner with someone outside the team to help build agendas and facilitate offsites, so that you can participate fully. At Return Path, we worked with executive coach Marc Maltz for almost the entire lifespan of the company. Marc helped us to build and adapt the leadership team over time, coached our CEO, individual team members, and the team as a whole.

Once you have a high functioning leadership team, it's much easier to build high functioning teams who report to them. Teams at the startup stage are often very cross-functional and the more you can help all individuals build the skills and practices to work effectively as team members, the faster they can make an impact on the teams that they join.

Picture a scaleup of 50 people. All employees report to a leadership team member. Some teams are small and each individual wears multiple hats. Even larger teams don't always have a standard role. Everyone knows each other. If these cross-functional teams don't have the skills to communicate with each other effectively, and they let their egos get in the way, even small conflict becomes painful and takes an emotional and productivity toll. If the teams all have the tools to set up effective operating systems and are able to communicate effectively, small conflicts can easily be handled between teams or people, making the team quickly productive.

For teams that work together regularly, treat them as an intact team, and follow the same steps from the "Five Dysfunctions" process that you did for the leadership team. Because all team members have a common language and skills, often the focus is on team dynamics and calling those to the surface. These skills also help teams be more inclusive. Working with people who come from different backgrounds and cultures requires more effective communication and inclusive practices such as ensuring that everyone has a chance to speak up at meetings, and that quieter people aren't ignored.

When team membership changes with a new hire or a change in role, take the opportunity to talk about your team operating system and dynamics and build new relationships and dynamics where appropriate. As Matt says, "Every time you add or lose a team member, you have a new team." At Return Path, we had every new employee take a Strengthsfinder assessment, and they used that to introduce themselves to the team. That helped to build trust quickly.

9

Leadership Development

As a startup, you generally aren't large enough to build or need a formal leadership development program. Work with the leadership team to ensure you are all aligned in expectations of leadership and management, and that each person on the leadership team is managing his or her own department effectively. Your role in a startup is still important and you need to drive conversations and learning and development around leadership skills so the leadership team is modeling strong leadership behavior to others in the organization.

You might have to coach the CEO and each leadership team member when you see or hear about behavior that doesn't align to values, and good leadership team members will appreciate that feedback in an honest and direct manner. We all have blind spots and identifying, giving feedback on, and helping leaders manage these blind spots early on will give you a good foundation on which to build. This can be difficult for you when it's the CEO or a cofounder who has a blind spot that impacts other people or when they act in ways that don't align with company values. These can be tough conversations, but if you have strong relationships and explicit permission to give feedback, your impact on the leadership team and the company can be significant.

As you grow beyond the ability of the leadership team to manage all direct reports, you'll need to hire managers and you'll need to develop and deliver management training for first-time managers. This is a prime opportunity for you to put in place the culture, values, operating system, and DE&I principles that will be the foundation with which you can scale quickly. Your management training needs to include necessary tasks such as approving expenses and PTO, managing compensation, and building an effective operating system, but it should be more than a list of do's and don'ts. You should also build leadership skills, such as emotional intelligence, listening, coaching, and having difficult conversations. You don't have to carry this weight alone. Ask leadership team members to develop and deliver training in their areas of expertise. This helps them deepen their skill and it gives them an opportunity to connect to the development of their team members and really embed the leadership behaviors that you want to reinforce.

As you scale, ensure you have enough People Business Partners (PBPs) to coach all managers across the organization. The PBP will help support managers' growth and development and continue to help you build your leadership bench. It takes a long time for a person to become a strong leader but you can shorten the path with intentional training, practice, and coaching. As you grow, many of the scaling practices in this section such as leadership development programs and leveraging volunteers across the organization can reduce your PBP:employee ratio.

In addition to training for managers, develop and deliver training on core leadership skills that you expect from every employee. Things like communication skills, interrupting unconscious biases, emotional intelligence, and receiving and giving feedback. When you help individuals develop these skills, the organization is better able to handle conflict and change. Collaboration, conflict, and decisions can be managed by the people closest to the problem, rather than needing to be escalated to formal leaders.

As you grow and start to hire second-level managers, you'll need to develop and deliver leadership training in the skills required to lead multiple teams. Emotional intelligence is even more critical here; the leader is even more in a "fishbowl" than first-level managers, as they are leading bigger teams or departments, and people have higher expectations of their standards of behavior.

When you get to this point, consider engaging an outside consultant or leadership development firm to support development and delivery. Ensure that the consultant is highly aligned with your values. Build and facilitate content together whenever possible; the consultant will have a big impact on your organization, since they will be impacting the people who role-model behaviors for others. At Return Path, we co-created one of our senior leader programs with the Refinery Group. Angela Baldonero, our Head of People at the time, worked very closely with them to ensure that they fully understood our culture, values, and leadership expectations. In addition to building high quality programs, the investment paid off in other ways: one of their consultants, Mark Frein, later became our Head of People, and another of their consultants, Russ Hamilton, later partnered with us to build communication and leadership skills throughout the company. The last program that we built with Russ, "Leading Teams," was one of the most impactful leadership programs we have ever experienced. The participants were from across the company, and the cohorts still regularly get together to connect and support each other, even though most no longer work together. See www.startuprev.com for a table showing the components of our leadership development at Return Path.

10

Talent and Performance Management

You have an opportunity early on to establish your philosophies around talent and performance. Help your leadership team understand the value of having open and honest communication around performance. Coach each leadership team member on having regular performance conversations with their team members so they are building skills and practices and modeling that behavior for future managers. Remember that in a startup it's likely that this is the first executive role for many on your leadership team and they haven't been groomed for years to hold that position. They're learning about the "art" of being an executive so you should help them understand how critical communication and listening are to being successful.

Run a semi-annual process to formalize performance conversations. These can be done on a form or shared spreadsheet, and can either be simple self:manager reviews, or can be more team-based. For the self:manager review, build in questions on career pathing to ensure that managers and employees are having conversations about professional development. It's not too early to groom your next leaders in the company, even though you won't yet have a formal career path laid out.

You can also build in questions for managers to get feedback from their employees.

Consistently evaluate what is and isn't working with your current feedback practices, and then modify the practices and build systems around them. Be creative and meet the needs of your organization. If you have a collaborative, transparent culture, you can implement team-based performance systems. Google published an article on its *Re: Work* site that talks about Return Path's innovative work around performance which we would recommend reading.[1] It highlighted our live 360° practices which were focused on team and individual performance and development. If your company is more hierarchical, you can implement more traditional systems based on annual goals and self:manager reviews. At Return Path, we iterated on our review process every year to make sure that the practices were still working effectively for individuals, teams, and the organization.

As you grow, build support tools for teams and employees, including manager training and guidelines and training for giving and receiving feedback, and developing high and low performers. Build manager guides and training on biased language and phrases to ensure inclusion. Performance reviews are a great example where unconscious bias can creep in, for example, women are often given critical feedback in reviews that they are too "aggressive" and men with the same behavior are given positive feedback for being "assertive" or a "leader." Having guidelines like these to help interrupt our own biases is a good example of a process change that supports DE&I.

Ensure you are capturing data in a way that allows you to evaluate your people and their talents across the organization, so that you can ensure you have the right people to support company growth and succession planning. Run semi-annual department and company-wide talent reviews to ensure high performers are recognized and developing and low performers are developing or managed out. As you grow, you'll want to

---

1. See https://rework.withgoogle.com/case-studies/return-path-team-effectiveness/

ensure that you have succession plans in place for all key executive roles, and a limited number of key senior, nonexecutive roles, where there is already a logical internal successor.

11

Career Pathing

To support both performance and professional development, first map out what it takes to be successful at different levels within your company, aligning these expectations to your values. You can do this by interviewing high performers and people who are aligned culturally. At Return Path, we had five "RP Expectations" articulated across four levels from entry level to executive. You can use these expectations in hiring, for performance conversations and to support career development. See www.startuprev.com for an example of the expectations at manager level, which includes development steps within each level. This may be too detailed for a raw startup; we crafted this when we had almost 100 employees. At Bolster, we've re-created leadership expectations for all executives, in addition to functional expectations at different stages of company growth, and built these frameworks into our software platform.

After you've mapped out expectations at a company level, collaborate with leaders in the largest departments and map out career frameworks for their teams. Ensure these are developmentally focused and clearly lay out what it takes to be successful in a role, and ready for promotion to the next level. Career pathing frameworks seem really hard for people to develop, possibly because roles change and if the framework is wrong, employee expectations aren't met. A good practice is to start simple, and continuously remind people that these are developmentally focused, will change over time, and are guidance only. The framework will show the difference in responsibilities and skills between the junior and senior roles on the team, as well as the compensation starting points for each role and geography. In sales, also include the quota for the new role. See www.startuprev.com for excerpts from Return Path's service roles.

Once you have frameworks in place for the largest department, it's really important to share these more broadly, as career paths are often more like a jungle gym than a ladder—people often benefit from moving across functions to broaden their skill sets, rather than always following a defined path.

To go along with your career pathing frameworks, document your promotion processes and practices. Generally, moving up within a role is different than being hired into an open position. For the former, have one to two cycles a year for these promotions. Be clear on the criteria for promotion. If you only need a certain percentage of the department to be in a senior role, let people know that they need to meet the criteria for the role *and* the business must have a need for it. When someone applies for and is offered a position in another department, the promotion should happen when the role opens rather than waiting for the next cycle. Having a strong practice around posting all openings internally along with a robust promotion process to move between levels in a job family, and requiring managers to have regular career pathing conversations with their teams, support employee retention, and diversity, equity, and inclusion. Without these processes, it is easy for leaders to sponsor people who are similar to themselves, and therefore give those individuals a better opportunity for promotion. Building systems and processes to interrupt our unconscious biases is a proactive step to building an inclusive culture.

12

Role-Specific Learning and Development

To support employees' success in their role and development into more senior roles, you will have to support development of job-specific skills. At early stages, teams aren't large enough to justify full training programs, and will benefit from having some of their repeatable practices documented, so before you hire a new employee onto a team, encourage the team to document their team's processes and practices, and this can be a starting point for building an informal training program.

For teams who are hiring more regularly or have skill development needs across a larger team, build training programs that start with the most critical role-specific skills. Identify and provide guidance to key employees who can mentor and train other employees. Often customer-facing roles need to be trained in your methodologies and in customer service skills. The training at this stage doesn't need to be developed or delivered by a learning professional, but can be enhanced with support from you or a PBP. When this work is more centralized, you get a perspective onto which skill development is needed more broadly across the organization.

As you grow, you may hire learning and development professionals onto your team, rather than relying on subject-matter experts on the functional team. This is another place that you can benefit from hiring an internal person who knows the business and is passionate about development, and then train them on learning and development practices.

When you get to this stage, step back and conduct a needs analysis across the organization, and partner with key departments to develop and deliver training programs. In some cases, you'll still use subject matter experts to deliver training, and in others, you'll build robust training programs that leverage online, in-person, and on-the-job modalities.

It's helpful to have a learning management system to track attendance and other key metrics so you can evaluate learning objectives and outcomes and adjust your programs as needed.

13

Employee Engagement

As a startup, with a handful of employees, it's easy to understand the pulse of the company, but as you scale, it's difficult to know whether values are guiding everyday behavior, and if there is alignment between the aspirational culture and the experience people have on the job. Initially, make sure you talk to employees regularly and surface any specific patterns of behavior to the leadership team. That can be difficult, especially if the feedback is about the leadership team behaviors. If this is the case, collect data in as objective a way as possible, and pull it together to share with the leadership team, rather than try to rely on just what you are hearing informally in the organization.

As soon as you are able to afford it, we recommend a robust employee survey tool such as Culture Amp or Emplify to help you understand your employees' experience. Both of these tools have banks of questions (so you don't have to create your own questions from scratch) and industry benchmarks. This will give you data to gauge the culture and values. This data can be used with the leadership team to create a formal organizational development plan. An organizational development plan is similar to a strategic plan, with the focus on the company—the people in it, their interactions, their working relationships, and their perspectives on how things are being managed—rather than on the business. For example, if you learn through an employee survey that managers aren't living the values, you can implement a management training program to improve manager skills, more clearly set out management expectations, and develop a manager scorecard to give managers feedback on how they are doing against those expectations. Or if you get data that one specific manager isn't living the values, you can provide coaching and their leader can start to monitor performance more closely.

Once you have a baseline of employee engagement, you can increase the cadence of your surveys by doing periodic shorter surveys or by adding department-specific development planning sessions. These are opportunities for teams and departments to evaluate how their team is doing and agree on a development plan to help them become a more effective team. This is a perfect opportunity to have a People Business Partner collaborate with the leader to run these sessions, and then coach the leader and the team in implementing their plan.

14

Rewards and Recognition

Think about the ways that you want to reinforce behavior and performance that contribute to your culture or your business. Build a simple recognition program that is aligned with your company values. Start with a manual system using your internal website or a form, unless you have a platform that offers this functionality. Just make sure to publicly recognize people for their contributions and allow peers a formal platform to say "thank you" and recognize each other's contributions.

At Return Path, we started our rewards system when the company was less than six months old with a wiki page showing six awards that aligned to our values, and every employee could give another employee recognition that came with a $25 reward. We manually processed the recognition part each week, and once a quarter sent a gift card to each employee with all their rewards. This worked for quite a long time, and only took a couple of hours each month and a few hours at year-end to manage. Later, we purchased a SaaS-based rewards system, and modified the program a little to encourage more cross-functional recognition.

As you expand, consider carefully what resonates with your values and culture. You may want to add team recognition and a more robust process for communicating recognition. Ensure that you have some guidelines in place to have equitable systems for different role or personality types. Not everyone likes public recognition, and people in client-facing roles are more likely to get recognition for small achievements than people in back-end roles like engineering. Use the same solution for all groups, so you can encourage cross-functional recognition, but be careful about too many rewards for the "most recognized" since that doesn't always reflect the highest performance or impact to the culture or company. Many companies have a sales awards program like a "President's Club." We have stayed away from those in favor of a system that recognizes people throughout the company, but they are popular awards with salespeople. At Return Path, we created an annual event called Performance Aspire that was a combination of development, fun, and networking for top performers across the organization, and attendees were selected after a peer nomination process from all departments. We had an amazing positive response from attendees, many of whom hadn't attended anything like that previously.

15

Reductions in Force

At any stage, when the business is not performing well, or if you've shifted your business strategy and completely changed what roles are needed, you may need to manage a reduction in force. The traditional way to manage this is to have the leadership team sit in a room with spreadsheets and talk about headcount. Maybe they engage leaders in the conversation to help build a change plan. They then go and execute the change plan, walking people out the door immediately after firing them. We've all either seen or heard about someone getting walked out the door with their box by a security guard. The problems with the traditional way of doing a reorganization is that:

- It doesn't allow for any input from employees.

- It treats people as if they can't be trusted.

- It doesn't give space for the people left behind to process departures.

- It doesn't allow for any type of transition.

Traditional executives often justify this approach by saying that they have to "pull the band-aid off" and that it's too risky to let terminated employees back to their desks. They'll say that it causes too much disruption to consult people ahead of time. The reality is that it's incredibly damaging to the trust and goodwill that you've built up with your employees if you treat a reduction or downsizing as a "headcount" issue. It takes a long time to regain the trust, confidence, and credibility of employees and make them believe that you are a people-centric and transparent organization if they come into an all-hands meeting one day and find boxes in the lobby and rent-a-cops on hand to escort people out the door, after being fired in a group setting. It's easy to treat people well when things are going well but it takes much more leadership courage to treat people well when things are going badly.

Some suggestions for managing this type of difficult change:

- Decide as a leadership team the overall strategic direction and budget going forward.

- Engage leaders in the conversation and ask them to help co-create a plan.

If there's any negotiation in who leaves and who stays, create a short process to consult with employees (noting that this is legally required in some countries):

- Let them know the rationale and strategy.

- Ask for input on what the employee wants (do they want the new role/voluntary redundancy/apply for a different role?).

- Make decisions, and communicate to impacted employees first in a one-to-one verbal communication (yes, I mean, not in an email or in a large-scale video call).

- Give all impacted employees a generous package that includes:

- ◦ Transition time: to transition their work and say goodbye to colleagues. Usually a week is sufficient, although some roles are much longer.

- ◦ A severance package.

- ◦ Career placement and continued severance if they can't find a job.

If you do this well, you'll reap the rewards in years to come. Return Path had a large layoff one year, and the next year, as the business grew again, we re-hired six people who had been laid off. All were excited to return, and that wouldn't have happened if we'd treated them poorly when they exited.

16

Recruiting

Your first priority is to work with the CEO/founders/leadership team to create the culture and values that define your company. Once those are established and communicated, you'll need to focus on recruiting. After you've hired your favorite former colleague, your CEO's brother-in-law, and your cousin's neighbor, you'll need to figure out where you'll find the rest of your people! Since there's so much work to do to build the People part of the business, it's likely that your first hire will do some recruiting, and your second hire will be a recruiter. You might even get a fractional or contract recruiter, until you know for sure you have enough work for a full-time role. We strongly suggest that you stay deeply engaged in recruiting efforts at this stage, especially for leadership roles since leaders have a far greater impact on the organization than new hires at other levels.

Thinking about the overall recruitment process, strategy, and approach your organization is going to take will be helpful to do up front. For example, will you have a strong customer service approach with your candidates and hiring managers or will it be a softer touch model? Do you plan to grow in one location or will you be open to employees working remotely or expanding to new geographies where talent pools might be stronger? There are pros and cons of different approaches and there is no one best way, but thinking through the time, resources, and outcomes for your recruitment strategy before it ramps up is critical.

You'll also want to think strategically about what type of talent your organization will want to hire. Do you need industry experience or specific skills and experience? If so, will hiring from your competitors be part of your overall strategy? Do you need everyone in one location? How many people will you need to bring in at one time? Understanding your talent needs, and being aligned with the leadership team and managers is an important driver of growth. All of these can also change over time—you might start out with hiring more experienced industry people and then move to a junior-hiring model when you get critical mass in a department. During the early stages, everyone you hire must be able to wear many hats as they'll all be doing multiple jobs. It's only when you scale that your employees will be able to separate into singular, focused roles. These early hires must also be flexible as priorities change frequently and they'll be pulled from one project or initiative to another.

It's essential that there is a values match between each new hire and the company. Once you have a values match, find candidates with diverse backgrounds and experiences. According to the *Wall Street Journal*, "the 20 most diverse companies in the research not only have better operating results on average than the lowest-scoring firms, but their shares generally outperform those of the least-diverse firms, the research shows" and, it's never too early to start. Your early hires are critical to your success as they are the most likely to be hired into or promoted within the organization to positions of leadership. If you want to give your company the best chance of success, make sure that new hires (especially executives) align on values with the CEO and company. If the CEO values transparency, for example, and another executive has a "need to know" attitude, the organization will reject that executive.

Like an Organ Transplant

I've often said that hiring a new senior person into an organization is a bit like doing an organ transplant. You can do all the scientific work up front to see if there's a match, but you never know until the organ is in the new body, and often some months have gone by, whether the body will take or reject the organ. New senior people in particular have a vital role in organizations. Often they are brought in to fix something that's broken, or to start up a new position that growth has created. Sometimes they are replacing a problematic person (or a beloved one). Usually, the hope is that they will also bring a fresh perspective and good outside view to bear on people whose heads are too much "in the business." In all cases, their role as leaders makes them have higher visibility and higher profile than most, and therefore more impactful if they succeed. It also makes them more problematic if they don't. What happens that causes the body to reject the organ? It could be a few things, but in my experience it's usually one of three. Sometimes the execution isn't there—in other words, the person knows what needs to be done but isn't effective in getting it done, for any number of reasons. Usually, you feel like you were sold a bill of goods. Other times, specifically in cases where the person is coming into a new job that didn't exist before, it turns out the job was poorly specified and doesn't need to exist, or that the person coming in is the wrong person for it. Usually, the person feels like they were sold a bill of goods. But I think in most cases, the cultural add just isn't there. And that's not really anyone's fault, although it "should be" something you can interview for to a large extent. These are the most painful ones to deal with. Decent to stellar execution (good enough to not end employment over it), but poor cultural fits. How quickly does this take? I've seen it take a quarter. I've also seen it take a year. But in both cases, the warning signs were there much sooner. A footnote on this is that as Return Path has grown, I've come to a new thought about this—it doesn't just apply to senior people. It applies to almost any new hire. It may be an outcome of having a really strong and consistent culture, or it may just be the natural extension of this axiom. **Matt Blumberg, *Executive Chair, Bolster***

We once had an open role for a senior leader on my team, who would be my manager. We knew that we needed someone who was process-oriented as that wasn't a strength of anyone on the team. We found and hired a person with that skill set even though we had some misgivings about this person's fit on the team; they seemed a little stiff, formal, and process-oriented for our environment. The misgivings were spot-on: the hire was a train wreck. While they did have the process-oriented skills we desperately needed at the time, they didn't share our values around people and actually had the opposite value! They valued process over people while we valued processes to support people. That mis-hire was highly impactful in the wrong direction. It set us back financially and emotionally, we squandered valuable time, and we almost lost at least one valuable leader before we made a decision to un-hire the mis-hire! We wasted a lot of time and resources in onboarding, evaluation of performance, and getting feedback from employees, and we created a lot of stress in the team. We learned a valuable lesson that it's absolutely necessary to pay attention to the person's values and not just their skill sets.

To determine values fit, we built interview guides against our Return Path Expectations to help interviewers with this assessment of whether the applicant exhibits the behaviors required at our company for the specific level of role. We also conducted reference checking for each senior hire. You'll want to dig deeply into the candidate's work style, communication strengths, and weaknesses, leadership, along with the technical skills needed for the role. Most importantly, make sure you understand whether a candidate shares your company values and whether they will be a culture add. (we are not fans of culture "fit" as it can unintentionally exclude people from different backgrounds, which reduces the diversity of your culture.) Without alignment on values and culture, you're doing a disservice to the potential new hire and you're hurting your company's chances of success.

Even at the startup stage you'll want to build a simple recruiting process that all candidates will go through, including structured or behavioral interviews. Even if you get resistance from frenzied hiring managers and executives, it's important to have a process that is consistent and lightweight, one that is inclusive (see www.startuprev.com for a DE&I chart with more specifics), and one that is efficient for the People team, hiring managers, and the candidate.

You will save a lot of time, energy, and frustration in the long run if you spend quality time planning for each hire. If you have good recruiting practices and processes, and use a tool like Gapjumpers, it could take as little as 15–30 minutes to whittle down hundreds of candidates to the top three who are likely to be successful in your company. Often every individual in a startup wants to interview every new hire. While that's admirable, it's unrealistic and you should highly discourage that. Instead, create a recruiting process such as the sample of the Interview Chart at www.startuprev.com.

You'll also want to build some basic approvals and tracking processes such as the sample of Recruiting Approvals and Tracking Processes at www.startuprev.com.

You'll also need to think about how you will source candidates. Often startups have a harder time attracting candidates because they aren't yet stable, known organizations, and there isn't an easy way for candidates to research what it's like to work for them. Many of your first hires may be sourced through internal referrals. While this is a good source of candidates, and you may be tempted to go with quick wins here, you have a real opportunity when you are small to build in diversity from the beginning, and sourcing from your internal referrals may limit your pool of diverse candidates. Once you've hired homogeneously for a long time, it's much more difficult to diversify your culture and your hiring. If you are hiring quickly, it can be helpful to supplement your team with an outside source, who knows your culture and value proposition well, and has the tools, resources, and experience in bringing you a strong and diverse candidate supply. Establishing a social media presence can create more name recognition and highlight your company as an employer of choice. So can having a presence and posting jobs with local meetups, startup events, universities, Indeed, LinkedIn, Twitter, Google Search or other more niche sites are useful. Look for automation in sourcing as a way to bring speed and efficiency to this process.

One way that we found a great talent pool was through the creation of a return-to-work program which targeted candidates who had taken time off work for caregiving, and then we supported them in their re-entry. If you get creative, there are a lot of people with potential to be successful in your company who don't have a "traditional" resume.

As the organization grows, as you go from a handful of employees to 100 or more, you'll need to add additional staff in the recruiting area and build more scalable processes. The stage when you need to take your team to the next level will be highly dependent on the employee growth plan. You'll have an understanding of your capacity for hiring, and you'll want to keep track of the strategic plan around hiring and growth, so you can build your team ahead of demand. At this stage, you will be using a lot of the same processes as before, but you'll ensure that the practices are all scalable.

For all your other processes, you'll start to move away from individual conversations with each hiring team. Instead, focus on building training and automated processes including hiring manager training that is mandatory for all interviewers. This can be a pre-recorded module or it can be an in-person class that you offer periodically. You can also write "how to" guides for managers to help them understand the recruiting process and their role in it. Take everything you've been telling hiring managers in one-to-one conversations and put it into a guide.

We prefer to be hands-on in recruiting, and to be highly involved and manage all recruiting in-house. The only exception is if we have overflow sourcing and there are times when you'll need to use outside recruiting agencies. It's worth developing relationships with a couple of local agencies and putting agreements in place before you need them. If you have a burst of hiring activity, you'll need to supplement your team with an agency that you trust, and who can bring you diverse candidates. Share your recruiting practices and processes with the agency and ensure they understand your culture and business.

As you grow, you'll need a coordinated effort to manage your employment brand. Although it's important at any stage to build a close partnership with Marketing in building the value proposition for talent, that work really pays off as you grow. Work with your internal marketing/corporate communications team to develop a full plan around employment branding, including partnering with sites that candidates use for research (i.e. Glassdoor, the Muse, Indeed, Built In). It's important to have a strong career site on your corporate website that features pictures and quotes from your employees, a clear Employee Value Proposition that you can advertise, and materials and swag for career fairs. Your career site will be a critical tool in your employment brand and should also include things like your values statement, benefits overview, what's great about working at your company, or any kind of content to showcase what an incredible culture and company you're creating or have created. Career sites allow candidates and former employees to leave comments about the company, and my approach is to use that feedback (especially if it's negative) for ways to improve your recruiting processes. We also responded to each comment publicly to make it clear that we heard and were working on the feedback.

At this stage of growth you may need highly specialized and hard-to-find positions, and we recommend posting your jobs to niche job boards. This is a great way to increase diversity in your talent pools. It's also possible to diversify your talent pool by participating in recruiting events, by sponsoring events that play to your company's needs (engineering fairs, pitch competitions, etc.) or by getting involved and sponsoring local community activities. You may meet with hundreds of people at local events and you might come back empty-handed, but you will have introduced your company and needs to many people who in turn are now able to articulate your company, vision, values, and needs to people in their network. Sometimes a wide net can generate qualified candidates reaching out to you.

There are a lot of details that go into creating a robust recruiting process and some metrics on the data you're collecting will help you both evaluate and improve your processes. Some sample metrics that are worth tracking include source data, cost per hire, time to fill a position, quality of people hired, first year attrition (both actual numbers and percentage), and candidate experience during the interview process.

Everything in this chapter has focused on external recruiting; earlier we talked about career pathing and promotions. Internal recruiting is hugely valuable; it's an important part of your growth to provide opportunities for your employees to map out their career. There's nothing quite so powerful as helping people develop skills, add responsibilities, and work with mentors to contribute to the company in greater capacity. At Return Path, we had a bias toward an internal promotion unless there were specialized technical skills that were lacking internally and we couldn't train. We then invested heavily in leadership development to help people grow and develop their careers. When Return Path was sold, the entire leadership team except the three initial founders had been promoted from within the company, thanks to a strong developmental focus and investment in people over the years.

17

Onboarding

One of the more people-focused roles within People Operations is onboarding. Effective employee onboarding is critical, even in startups. Most people think of onboarding as getting a benefits overview and a computer. That's important, but that's really just "orientation." The first experiences an employee has with your company will help determine longer-term success. With a small team you may not have time to create a fully curated and personalized experience for every new employee; instead, put some structures in place to ensure hiring managers and teams are creating that great experience for new hires.

As you start to increase hiring, you can build a more robust onboarding program so that each manager doesn't have to re-create a program for their new employee. The onboarding manager can be responsible for setting up the programs that will be run for all employees, and then build manager and new employee guidelines that give them each a framework for job- and company-specific activities and outcomes in the first 90 days. In addition to building the guidelines, the onboarding team can manage or collaborate with other teams to manage things such as:

- Training in soft skills that are critical to success at your organization as discussed in leadership development above.

- First day setup. You don't want people to show up and no one knows who they are or to have to put a desk together. Get buy-in from office management so they understand the impact that the first day setup can have on the employee experience, and are creating a great experience for each new employee.

- A way for new employees to be introduced to the company, whether that's a welcome email to the entire company or a short bio shared on TV screens, helping new employees introduce themselves in a non-threatening way, and also letting colleagues learn about them before they meet in person.

- Programmatic story-telling sessions led by the CEO and senior leaders to deepen employees' understanding of values and bring them to life.

- 90-day reverse review process, where the CEO or member of the leadership team talks to the employee one-to-one about their first 90 days. This is a good way for the leaders to develop connections with employees, get ideas from them while they are still learning, and also get feedback about the recruiting and onboarding process. It also highlights for leaders that personal engagement with employees is really important.

- A "buddy" program to connect a new and an experienced employee to answer questions, and help the new employee integrate effectively.

- A unique onboarding process including job-specific training for departments that have a significant number of people in the same role.

Onboarding vs. Waterboarding

A senior hire once said to me that they enjoyed our onboarding process during the first 90 days at Return Path and that at other companies the first few months were more like waterboarding.

We placed a lot of emphasis on onboarding—the way we asked employees to spend their first 90 days on the job. I've often said that the hiring process doesn't end on the employee's first day. I think about the employee's first day as the midpoint of the hiring process. The things that come after the first day—orientation (where's the bathroom?), context-setting (here's our mission, here's how your job furthers it), goal setting (what's your 90-day plan?), and a formal check-in 90 days later—are all make-or-break in terms of integrating a new employee into the organization, making sure they're a good hire, and making them as productive as possible.

- Nothing has a greater impact on a hire's long-term viability than a thorough onboarding and if you don't onboard them properly, they may never work out. This is where all companies, big and small, fail most consistently. Remember your first day of work?

- Did you (or anyone at the company) know where you were supposed to sit?

- Did you (or anyone at the company) know if your computer was set up?

- Did you (or anyone at the company) have a project ready for you to start on?

- Did you (or anyone at the company) know when you'd be able to meet your manager? Probably not.

Take onboarding *much* more seriously, and you'll be astounded by the results. We had a Manager of Onboarding whose only job was to manage the first 90 days of every employee's experience. If you don't have a manager for onboarding, here are some things you can, and *must*, do to assure a successful onboarding process:

1. Start onboarding before Day 1. Ask new hires to create a "Wall Bio"—a one-page collage of words and images that introduces them to the team—before their first day.

> 2. Set up your new hire's desk in advance, including their computer, monitor, telephone, nameplate, and company swag.
>
> 3. Prepare an orientation deck, one-to-one, or session for Day 1 including mission, values, structure, and strategic plan.
>
> 4. Clearly set 90-day objectives and goals including the new hire's job description, first steps they should take, resources they should know, people they should meet, training courses to take, and their major objectives for their first 90 days.
>
> 5.Run a review process at the end of 90 days.
>
> With *that*, the hiring process is done. Now, repeat. **Matt Blumberg,** ***Executive Chair, Bolster***

See www.startuprev.com for an example of first day/first week minimum requirements for new hires.

18

Compensation

You'll want to develop a basic compensation philosophy and make sure there is alignment with the leadership team. While benefits and other non-monetary perks such as company culture factor into your overall Employee Value Proposition, for this chapter I'll focus on financial compensation. Compensation is both an art and a science, and people often have strong perspectives about how to compensate employees, and have strong emotions attached to this. If you aren't aligned with your leadership team and CEO, you'll spend a lot of time on this topic for new hires and during compensation reviews and promotions.

We recommend aligning on the following questions around your compensation philosophy and how you'll make decisions:

- How will you compete in the market on compensation? Will you pay below, at, or above market rates for base compensation?

- Will you have a commission plan for sales?

- Will you have a bonus plan for employees?

- Will you give stock options to all employees?

- How often will you review compensation and consider promotional increases? Will you pull out junior roles and do more frequent reviews for those positions whose market rate can change more quickly?

- Who is responsible for compensation decisions? Is it the Chief People Officer or the functional executive?

- How will you handle geographic differences in market compensation? Will you pay different amounts in your different locations?

- How transparent will you be about compensation? Will you tell everyone your philosophy, salary bands for each role, or every individual employee's salary?

- How will you handle executive compensation?

Collaborate with your recruiting team to understand the market, and determine rates for specific roles based on your philosophy. Once you have the starting pay rates for specific roles, set a no-negotiation policy, especially for junior roles. A no-negotiation policy will help keep compensation equitable across people and roles and will also speed up the recruiting process since it eliminates the back and forth between you and the potential new hire.

On Decision Making

It's a good practice to have final compensation decisions made by a small corporate committee, consisting of the CEO, the CFO, and the CPO. This allows for more consistency and equity across the organization. In the last couple of review cycles I (Cathy) managed, the People team made all compensation recommendations based on our reviews of internal and market data. Managers weighed in on role changes and promotions, and we had more levels within each role with specific salary starting points, which allowed us to focus primarily on promotions and market adjustments, rather than performance. This reduced a lot of the friction in the organization, and allowed managers to focus their efforts on performance and development.

19

People Operations

While focusing on the culture and company you are trying to build, finding the right people to help you, and building systems to keep track of everything, you also need to focus on the transactional aspects of the function. These two broad areas—transactional work and culture—reinforce each other and as a startup it's best to create both of them in tandem. All aspects of transactional work will be influenced by company values and when you're growing rapidly it's tempting to recruit strong transactional people to the company right away. There are lots of people with the traditional skill sets, but being intentional about building the People Operations team sets the company up for rapid growth. Building the People Operations team with an Employee Value Proposition (EVP) mindset will help you develop effective processes, set the stage for long-term growth, and attract the people you'd want in People Operations. The EVP is a broad term for the entire employee experience and in a nutshell answers the question, "What can the employee expect to gain by working at your company?" That answer is the foundation of your employment brand, which is not set in stone on Day 1, and rather changes as you grow. The EVP includes values and cultures, which can play a big role in why someone wants to work at your company.

Again, even while it may seem urgent to just get payroll and benefits started, you'd do well to consider your EVP even in the very beginning. Your EVP will change over time as you mature, as you have more resources, or even as you respond to the market through new offerings, strategic partnerships, or other growth models. Many startups initially start with lower base compensation and higher equity. That's great if you have a small number of employees, but what happens once you have hundreds of employees? What equity amount will you need to compensate for low salary? Other companies provide great benefits (over higher compensation or equity) to attract new employees. Some companies have low benefits to reduce per-employee investment. Any of these approaches can work, as long as it's aligned with your values and the EVP is clearly stated.

Setting up the operational side of HR can be thankless work. People only notice when things go wrong—and they will let you know! Many leaders treat People Operations as a necessary evil, as a cost-center that either needs to be done in-house or outsourced, and rarely as a valuable asset to the company. It's your job to help people see operations differently and if you help people change their perspective about this, if you can get them to think of People Operations as a key contributor to your Employee Experience journey, this work can be more rewarding and impactful. Our former colleague, Amanda, mentioned earlier, is a great example of taking a transactional role and making it people-centric. Amanda joined the People Team as Payroll Coordinator, a highly transactional role, but she changed what had been a transactional, reactive role into a proactive, people-focused role. Amanda created and modified processes to be more people friendly and effectively communicated changes that impacted employees. The impact on the company was huge and we'd urge you to hire people who care about the people they are serving, even if the role is largely administrative or data-intensive. Sometimes, the best People Operations team members don't have HR backgrounds. They are interested in the work, passionate about helping people, and capable of doing that from a transactional role.

As you grow, you'll want to gain efficiencies with your People Operations, so they can serve a larger population without growing the team; otherwise you can easily become bloated, move too slowly, and not offer enough value to the company. If you are using a professional employment organization (PEO), you should regularly re-evaluate it to make sure it still meets your needs and budget. Often, companies bring payroll and benefits in-house when they reach 100 employees. If you are hiring in multiple countries, you may want to use a PEO in each country until you get enough employees there to justify an entity. Make sure that your broker relationships are still effective and that they know about your growth plans. The best brokers will be an extension of your team so if they aren't providing what you need, give them clear guidance on your expectations and be ready to find someone else if their business model doesn't match your needs.

Be creative about benefits—keep on top of trends, and talk to your employees about what is important to them. Some things we had at Return Path over the years were:

- Open vacation

- Sabbatical program

- Extended parental leave

- Well-being day

- Payroll and insurance benefits.

Open Vacation

We realized that people's work and lives were becoming more inter-twined, with work sometimes needing to be done on vacation time, and personal things needed to be done during work, and so we created an open vacation practice. With this, it meant a reduced administrative burden on tracking paid time off (PTO) balances. Employees could use PTO flexibly and could choose increments other than ½ or full days. We also included some guidelines for employees, like average and minimum annual PTO, approvals for longer than two weeks' PTO, and perfor-mance. You want to ensure that there's a balance between people and teams and that there are not abuses of its use. In many countries other than the US, you can use the "open/flexible" philosophy, but statutory leaves are usually sufficient.

Open Vacation: Was It Worth It?

At Return Path, we had an "open vacation" policy for years, meaning that we didn't regulate the amount of time off people took, and we didn't accrue for it or pay out "unused" vacation if someone left the company. I still get asked about this all the time, so I thought I'd give a couple of follow-up questions I usually get asked about it, and my response.

The first question I always get is, "Wow—does that really work? What issues have you had with it?"

No issues with it at all, other than it's a little weird to apply internationally, where we have 50 people across seven countries, since most of those countries have significantly more generous vacation policies/customs than the US. But we generally make it work.

The second question I get is whether people abuse it or not:

In all the years we've done it, we only ever had one person attempt to abuse the policy, one time. People do still have to ask their managers if it's OK to take time off, and they do still have to get their jobs done.

Finally, people ask me for general advice on implementing this kind of policy:

Continue to track days off and generate reports for managers every quarter so they at least know whether their people are taking not enough or too much—generally people will take not enough, and you will need to encourage them to take more. Also, our managers were "really" worried about launching this, so we had to do some hand-holding along the way.

My thoughts: The results of this policy for us have generally been great. People take about the same amount of true vacation they used to take, maybe a little more. They definitely take more half-days and quarter-days where they probably still get a full day worth of work done, without worrying about counting the hours. Best of all, there's a strong signal sent and received with this kind of policy that we trust our team members to do what they need to do in order to live their lives AND get their jobs done. **Matt Blumberg,** *Executive Chair, Bolster*

Sabbatical Program

Creating a sabbatical program early on is a good retention tool. Our initial sabbatical program was six weeks after seven years of service; we changed this to four weeks for every four years of service, which I'd recommend. The benefit is really appealing to employees, and it's also good for the company. When someone takes an extended leave from their job, they have to train others, and it often exposes single points of failure. It also gives others opportunities to stretch into new roles for a short period. When I took my sabbatical (an amazing trip to New Zealand and Australia—a once-in-a-lifetime opportunity), I trained others on the team on every aspect of my job and essentially didn't have a job to return to. That gave me the opportunity to lead a large-scale agile transformation project across the organization. Many people had a new lease on life and their job when they returned from sabbatical. And, we had a lot of fun celebrating people's return. Our President had his entire office filled with balloons from top to bottom, and many people left their "welcome back" artifacts in their cubes for months after their return.

Sabbatical: Was It Worth It?

I've written a few times over the years about our sabbatical policy at Return Path, and people ask me about our policy all the time. While it's not necessary to share every detail of the policy, a few specifics can be helpful.

The two biggest priorities in having a sabbatical are: (1) to ensure that people actually take advantage of this benefit, and (2) to ensure that people communicate and prepare for an extended absence. Here's a short list of "pre-sabbatical" tasks for employees and their managers.

As the employee

- Prepare your team. Make sure your goals and metrics for your time out are super clear and clarify who others should contact in your absence. Set expectations of management for coverage and look to see how your team members can take over some of the responsibilities. Give them stretch goals while you're out!

- Prepare your individual contributor work. Hand off all loose ends with extra details and make introductions via email if your manager/team member is going to have to work with external parties.

- Prepare your manager. Brief your manager thoroughly on everything going on with your team, its work, your individual contributor work, including one-to-one check-ins. Agree on a plan for coverage of team activities, one-to-ones, and big initiatives.

- Prepare yourself. Figure out how to keep your work and personal communications separate—your email (autoresponder, routing, disabling from your smartphone), your voicemail if you use Google Voice or Simulscribe, etc. Block out two full days immediately when you return to catch up on email and catch up with your manager and team. Plan any personal travel early so you get good rates!

As the manager

- Prepare your team. Figure out what kind of coverage you need (either internal or external) while you're covering and make sure the rest of your team knows your time will be compromised while you're covering. Rearrange your calendar/travel and add new team meetings or one-to-ones as it makes sense. You don't have to do exactly what your employee did, but some portions of it will make sense to pick up, and if your employee works in another office with members of their team, you might want to plan some travel there to cover in person. Remember to undo everything when the employee's sabbatical is over.

- While you're in charge. Learn as much as you can by doing bits and pieces of their job. This is a great opportunity for the employee to get some value from a fresh perspective. Surprise your employee with how much you were able to keep things running in their absence!

- Prepare for your employee's return. Keep a running tab of everything that goes on at the company, critical industry news (if appropriate), and with your employee's function or team and prepare a well-organized briefing document so your employee can hit the ground running when they return. Block out an hour or two each of the employee's first two days back to review your briefing document.

My main takeaway from this advice? I am overdue for my second sabbatical, and it's time to start thinking about that! **Matt Blumberg, *Executive Chair, Bolster***

Extended Parental Leave

While many countries other than the US already offer generous parental leave, we found that our employees really valued the extended paid time we offered for new parents. Initially, only employees with six months service were eligible. And then we had a new employee whose wife had a baby in his first six months at Return Path. His manager argued strongly for the employee to be offered the leave. The manager had recently taken parental leave and realized that it was important for him personally, and also helped him be more focused when he returned to work. We modified the program so that everyone was eligible.

Well-being Day

Every employee could select one from a variety of well-being packages each year. These packages were negotiated specifically for our employees, and included things like sessions with a nutritionist, a financial advisor, or a meditation coach.

Payroll and Insurance Benefits

There are some more transactional things you'll have to think about immediately in building out People Operations:

- As a startup you can either set up a simple payroll system such as Gusto, or contract with a professional employment organization (PEO).

- A PEO is a co-employer that manages all your payroll and benefits, which can save you time and money while you are small. They bring the benefits of economies of scale, as they are co-employers with many different companies. Their benefits can be more robust and affordable than what you can get as a single company, and they can ensure you are in compliance with all appropriate regulations and reporting requirements. The downsides to a PEO are that you lose some control of the employee experience and it can be expensive.

- If you don't use a PEO, evaluate your options and select and implement a simple payroll system. You'll want to ensure that the system can effectively onramp employees without manual intervention, and also collect some data that you can report on, such as employee turnover.

- If you don't use a PEO, evaluate and contract with a good benefits broker. A good broker will help you strategically and also tactically. They will help educate you about benefits options, understand your EVP, and advise on options that will support that. A benefits broker will also be a liaison to employees so you don't spend all your time answering benefits questions.

Processes

- Set up simple processes for collecting and making payroll changes. When you are small, you may get verbal requests for changes, and you should send a request by email so that you can track approvals for the changes. This is important for audit purposes and also ensures that your data is accurate and has the appropriate approvals. You'll need to work with Finance to determine payroll roles and responsibilities. The People Team is generally responsible for keeping employee data and responsible for ensuring any changes are accurately reflected. Finance is generally responsible for setting up tax entities, filing taxes, and processing payroll. A simple tracking system such as a shared Google sheet can be used to communicate and double-check payroll and benefits changes.

    - Leave of absence practices such as family/medical leave, parental leave and disability leaves are becoming more complex, and you'll need to understand required leaves of absence for each country and state in which you operate. The Society for Human Resource Management (SHRM) is a good resource for this type of information. Once you understand the laws, you'll need to understand how the leave is paid and communicated to different agencies. Sometimes your broker will help with these calculations, and if one of your vendors offers leave processing, it's a benefit you should take advantage of.

- ○ Create a simple process for collecting paperwork for employee files. Keep as much electronically as possible, working with IT to ensure that you have the appropriate level of security on those files. There are still requirements in some countries for paper files, so check requirements in each of your geographies.

Employee Documents

For new hire documentation, there are some new employee forms that are required by law, such as tax and employment eligibility forms. For the others, you have options for the presentation. If you look for standard forms online, you'll find a lot of them are written from a legal perspective. If you are trying to create a culture of trust in your organization, these aren't the best forms to start the relationship with. You need to understand what's required to protect the company (such as making sure it's clear that you are an "at will" employer in the US), and add those components to your paperwork. Write your offer and corresponding onramp documents in a conversational tone, welcoming your employee and giving them the information they need to be successful and excited about this move.

- • If you decide that you need legal documents such as non-disclosure, inventions, non-competes and non-solicits, you will want to leave in the more formal legal language. Think carefully about which of these protections you really need, and which are enforceable in your locations. As you grow, it can be helpful to have clarity around what you expect of employees, and a basic form with all these common restrictions is fairly common. Non-competes are becoming less enforceable in some locations, unless the role is a very senior role and the individual is being compensated for not working.

- Your employee handbook can also be written in a conversational tone. Most companies find that some form of handbook is really useful, and many of the policies included are required by law, but that doesn't mean that you have to write it in legalese, like my boss at the truck stop wanted. Most sample employee handbooks will be full of legal information and written as "rules" people have to follow but most of these sections are irrelevant (and can be removed), while others need to be rewritten from legal to conversational language. So, while you need an employee handbook, you don't have to make it difficult for people to understand. At Return Path we called our employee handbook the "People Pact" and it's available to view on our website.

Office Management

Whether it reports to you or not, office management plays a big role in the employee experience. If you're starting up a good idea is to fold Office Management into People Operations and if you're at a later stage of growth and Office Management is not reporting to you, we would strongly advocate for that to happen. The impact of Office Management goes far beyond the person sitting at the front desk greeting visitors. Over the past few years, more and more companies have been moving toward remote-first environments, and your People Operations and Office Management team can help facilitate remote employees' success. The COVID-19 pandemic is already making many companies rethink their Office Management strategies.

- Your CEO, founders, and leadership team should have a clear idea on whether or not you will be office-based as a result of their work on values and culture. If you are working in one location but expand to others we recommend that you immediately become "remote-first." That means that you will set up your processes and practices assuming that you won't be connecting in person. There are a lot of tools available to help employees stay connected and help managers keep track of progress, like Asana, Slack, and Zoom.

- If you're office-based, you'll want to collaborate with others on the office layout. If you're a company that collaborates, then you'll probably want flexible space for meeting and desks that can easily be moved so that you can work together. If you are hierarchical, you may want offices for all managers and if you aren't hierarchical, you may want to save all office space for collaborative meeting rooms.

- If you are remote-first, you'll most likely have employees come into any location only occasionally, and you might want to set up a lot of areas for video-conferencing in offices, especially for ad hoc meetings. You'll also probably want to develop a plan for desk-sharing,

- In today's environment it's expected that companies will provide food and drinks to employees and you'll have to decide on those. Since you'll also own any Well-being offerings, we'd suggest offering healthy snacks and food.

20

Systems

As you grow, you'll want to evaluate all your current systems and practices to ensure they are scalable. If you are growing quickly, inadequate systems will become a roadblock on your team's success and will fuel frustration in the organization. Your Human Resource information system (HRIS)/payroll system should be more robust so that you can seamlessly integrate with other systems such as your applicant tracking system (ATS). At this stage you should start to invest in greater functionality in your systems, such as performance and compensation management. Those things can quickly get unwieldy and cumbersome to run without a system that scales with you. You'll also want to start reporting on KPIs (key performance indicators) and employee metrics so you can monitor your employee data and catch any trends. You'll look at data over time like employee turnover, employee engagement, performance, revenue per person, and compensation equity.

As you start to grow, you'll need to ensure that all your systems are integrated. Often HR systems have single functions, but to get the best of that functionality, you'll need a standalone system for each. (This is changing and there are now systems that bring best-of-breed in multiple functions together.) By integrating several processes you'll reduce duplicate work for the People Operations team. When you are smaller, you can manually handle this work; as you get bigger, you'll want to streamline so you don't make mistakes and can leverage your team for more high-impact work. See www.startuprev.com for guidelines about systems to consider.

III. CPO AND THE LEADERSHIP TEAM

21

How to Hire a Chief People Officer

Cathy Hawley

In an earlier chapter on team building I suggested that in a startup it is often best to hire people who are comfortable wearing multiple hats, comfortable with uncertainty, and to hire people who complement you. And the reason for that is because there aren't developed processes and procedures, there isn't the capacity for the startup to have specialized roles, and everyone needs to be able to help out as things crop up. I also said that you often need to hire people before you grow because waiting for revenues and then hiring means that you're always playing catch up, you're always scrambling and putting your startup's growth in peril.

But once you get more consistent revenues, once you have some processes and systems in place, it might be time to look for a Chief People Officer. I have found that the right Chief People Officer for a startup is highly dependent on the type of business that you are operating and the nature of work that will be required. In the People side of the business there are three general areas that define most work, what I refer to as traditional HR leader, talent acquisition leader, and people and culture leader. I refer to those three areas as *personas,* because they broadly describe the type of person who will lead your HR/People & Culture department. The right Chief People Officer for your startup depends on what *persona* closely matches your situation. Are you in a highly competitive market for top tier talent? Then you should look for a talent acquisition leader. Is your company in an industry that requires more compliance or manufacturing? A traditional HR leader might be best. And if you are building an organization with numerous highly differentiated skillsets and backgrounds of employees, and you have a strong desire to build a great culture as well as a great company, then a people and culture leader might be best. Hiring the right Chief People Officer is dependent on the nature of work required as well as the phase of growth of your company and the speed of your scaling, and so the first broad question to think through and consider is the nature of your business and the type of work required by the CPO.

Persona Attributes and How to Find These People

At the Chief People Officer level it's likely that any candidate will have some experience or familiarity with all three *personas,* but each person will also likely have more experience, talent, and skills in one of the *personas.* A traditional HR leader / people operations leader will often have a more linear HR career path, and have a career more focused on the fundamentals of HR. A traditional HR leader will probably have an advanced degree, maybe a degree in HR, or they will have progressive experience in HR. Another quality of the traditional HR leader is that they will have owned people operations, or they will have been a leader of some other part of HR like compensation & benefits, learning & development, organizational design, or possibly HR business partners. You should also expect that a traditional HR leader will have a strong focus on operational excellence, which includes experience creating processes and practices that are scalable.

If you're using LinkedIn, a different platform, or an executive recruiter for a traditional HR leader, look for people with a career path starting out in roles such as HR coordinator, HR manager, or senior director of HR. You might also see people with HR business partner titles or people operations titles. The traditional HR leader will have a track record of significant leadership positions in multiple HR functions including People Operations, compensation and compliance..

If your Chief People Officer needs to scale the organization quickly then a talent acquisition leader is what you should look for. A person with significant experience in talent acquisition will most likely have started their career as a recruiter and then moved into HR. Within HR, this person should have owned talent, talent and retention, or sometimes on-boarding or people operations. On LinkedIn or other platforms, look for people who have had the title of recruiter first, and then people operations, second.

If your desire as a CEO is to build a great culture, because that fits your personal mission or because that's the type of company you need to attract the right talent, then a people and culture leader may be what you need. Finding a people and culture leader is not as clear-cut as finding a traditional HR leader or a talent acquisition leader because the people and culture leader may have a more diverse career path. Of course, they may have followed a traditional HR path, but it is also likely that they followed a path that includes learning and development or organizational development or maybe within HR they were involved in the people business partnership role. Like the other Chief People *personas,* the people and culture leader will have owned one or several functions within HR, like learning & development (including leadership / management development), organizational design, internal communications, culture, HR or people business partners, or people operations. This *persona* may also come from another part of the business; someone who knows the business well, and has passion about scaling the people function to meet business goals. That person would partner with a strong but more junior People Operations leader.

If you are looking on LinkedIn or any other platform to find a people and culture leader, look for people who started their career in roles such as HR coordinator, HR manager, Senior director HR (Or People or People Operations), or training coordinator. As they gain more experience, look for people that have HR business partner titles or learning and development titles. One other quality of a people and culture leader is that they should mention somewhere in their profile that they were a trusted advisor to the CEO and other executives. The people and culture leader puts a primacy on building a great culture and they will highlight that, along with something around "trusted advisor" in their profile.

When is the right time for this *persona*?

Once you figure out which *persona* you need for your company, the next problem to solve is, *when* do you hire this person? I'd suggest that the CEO have a partner who knows about People/HR from the very beginning. This might be a co-founder who has some background in People/HR, or an advisor. Then, start to scale this function through the use of fractional resources until you are big enough to need a full time Chief People Officer. Timing is company-dependent, but a good rule of thumb is that you'll need some kind of "head of" people leader around 50 people, and a full time CPO by the time you are 150 employees. If you are growing fast or have another complexity such as an all-remote workforce, or multiple countries that you serve, you'll want to hire full time sooner.

General questions to ask in interview

If you get to the interview stage with a Chief People Officer candidate it's always good to have a couple of probing questions you can refer to. Regardless of *persona,* these questions will provide a bit more background about the candidate, what they have been involved with, and how they think about problems.

- What was your mandate when you joined the business?

- How big was the business when you joined and where is it today? Here I would ask for the last 2-3 companies.

- What are the KPIs (key performance indicators) that you use to measure the company's culture, engagement, or other measures of health?

- When you joined "XXX," what was in place? What systems did you implement?

- "Tell me about a conflict you've had with another executive. What was the situation, the resolution, and your role in it?" Here I would listen for their ability to address conflict, understand their own triggers, have emotional intelligence around the situation, and effectively resolve it. You'll also get an understanding of the areas they are most passionate about. You can also ask about a time where they coached a peer.

- "Tell me about the relationship with your last CEO. Share a time that you disagreed about an approach or a strategy, and how you resolved that conflict. Tell me about a time you had to share difficult feedback with them."

You can probe a little further and ask, "Tell me about a large impact you made on an organization - what was the situation, the solution, and your role in the solution?" You can then ask a few *persona*-specific questions. For a traditional HR *persona*, ask more about operational effectiveness and knowledge of HR law and compliance focus. For a talent acquisition *persona*, ask more about building an employer value proposition, sourcing and recruiting strategy. For a people and culture *persona*, ask more about their experience building a great culture, and how they partner with and coach the CEO and executive team.

When you ask these questions, you ought to hear from the traditional HR *persona* something from them that demonstrates that they have the ability to understand the different functions within the HR team, how they operate together, and ability to build efficiencies. You would expect the answer to focus on operational effectiveness and the ability to take complex situations and build processes and practices to address the situations. A talent acquisition leader ought to respond with something that demonstrates their ability to source and engage talent, and understand the talent landscape. Finally, a people and culture leader responding to that question ought to bring up something that demonstrates that they understand how people function and operate and understand the business and how people impact the business. You should expect their answer to focus on cultural and people impact of decisions as well as business impact. For example, they might talk about executive team functioning but if they don't, you should follow up and ask them specifically what their role was within the executive team and what interactions they had with the executive team, such as coaching. You really want to understand whether the candidate is going to follow direction and be reactive, or be a strong strategic CPO.

A good follow-on question to ask is, "How did you use data to inform your solution and decision making?" I would leave this question open-ended but listen for answers that may include data and metrics around performance management, turnover rates, diversity, compensation planning, or other key HR metrics.

Your Choice

Although hiring a Chief People Officer involves understanding the various HR *personas* and skills, there are no hard rules or absolutes and the choice is entirely up to you. The interview questions suggested are merely that–suggestions to get the conversation going so that you can help a candidate speak authentically and candidly about their career and aspirations, and so that you can determine their readiness for a Chief People Officer role in your company. The best Chief People Officer will be able to come into your company and make an immediate impact. Understanding where your company is today and what you aspire to become in the future will help you identify, source, and hire a Chief People Officer who can do that. I have stressed throughout this book that a values-based, culture-driven organization can have enormous business benefits and that is something that can be achieved regardless of the *persona* you hire, although it's an easier path with a Chief People Officer who has the background noted in the People and Culture *persona*. So, I would explore each candidate's openness to building values and culture as the foundation for your company.

22

How I Work With the Leadership Team

Cathy Hawley

The most important and difficult part of the CPO role is influencing others. You'll influence others every day, from helping executives align with the People strategy that will drive their business, to helping employees think differently about the social contract, to helping managers think differently about what it means to manage and lead. You will do this every single day, in small and big ways.

To be successful, you need a really strong, trusting relationship with the CEO, and you need to understand where your values, strategy and practices are aligned with theirs, and where they differ. You cannot drive a People strategy that doesn't align with the CEO or the business. This is the first place you'll need your influencing skills. And, by this, I don't mean just convincing someone that they are wrong. I mean being able to synthesize multiple perspectives, experiences and opinions, including your own, and helping others understand your thought process, your recommendations, and your solutions.

Your relationship with the CEO is not only the most critical but also the most complex. You are both a direct report and a trusted advisor. 90% of the time, the latter relationship takes precedence. You are a confidante, a sounding board, reflector of feedback from the organization, a cultural steward, a team coach, and an individual coach. It's a very complex role - you have to be brave and push back when appropriate, be the messenger of performance feedback, run performance and 360 reviews, and have difficult conversations - all while maintaining a strong and trusting relationship. In some cases, you'll also have relationships with board members, especially if you have a compensation committee. In this case, you might also share insights about board performance or dynamics with the CEO.

You'll also need good relationships with the remaining executive team members. Even if you have a People Business Partner who supports each executive, you need to form and maintain your own relationships. You need to understand their mental models about culture and organizations, their past experience, and their priorities so you can best support and influence them. The most important relationships are with the executives who run the largest organizations at your company, usually CRO and CTO, and with other 'corporate' executives such as CFO and GC.

For the CXOs leading the largest organizations, you should understand the work that your team is doing in support of these priorities - everything from recruiting to team development to career pathing to compensation. I'd expect the PBP to 'own' the relationship and day-to-day tactics, and the CPO to track progress, remove roadblocks, and stay in alignment as priorities change. There will also be times where you'll perform some of the work, where you don't have senior enough people in those roles. For example, you might support executive hiring or leadership team development. For the 'corporate' executives, in addition to the above work, you'll work closely to ensure alignment on things like budget, metrics, compensation, systems and legal risk.

When you don't have good relationships, and don't try to understand the other CXO perspectives, your team will have a hard time being successful, as they'll have to go back and forth to ensure they are meeting both your goals, and the CXO's goals. This happened to me when I was trying to change our compensation philosophy to be more equitable. I insisted that all entry level jobs have a 'no negotiation' rule. My team would try to enforce this, but one executive kept making offers with different starting salaries for the same role. But until I was able to align our philosophies, I was not setting my team up for success.

To be successful as a CPO, you need to be a trusted advisor to the CEO and to the rest of the executive team. You don't always have to agree, but you do have to align. You also need to be courageous, and sometimes put your personal fear of saying the hard truths and damaging a relationship aside for the good of the company.

23

Fractional Chief People Officer

Courtney Graeber

I've been working in human resources and operations for over 20 years and I feel like all the positions that I've been in have been positions of transformation, where a company would bring me in at the beginning of something that needed to be changed. Maybe it was with an early-stage startup with no systems or processes in place, or a company that needed to pivot, or an organization that really wanted to do some kind of transformation of the business. What I've learned is that whether you're in a startup or in a larger organization that's looking for change, a lot of the characteristics and qualities are similar.

One thing I realized about myself is that what really got me excited was working with startups. I enjoy the infancy stages of a company and everything that goes along with it, like the wacky space, the weird furniture, and the people doing everything even though they don't know what they're doing. I'm excited by the messiness, the passion of the founders and I just want to get in there and make it all work.

Fractional HR Tasks

I recently wrapped up an assignment with a startup that provides an example of what a fractional executive does and the value they can bring. I got a call from someone who I used to work with who started a company and said, "We're in big trouble and we need you to help us out." Originally, they just wanted an HR presence that would help employees if there were any employee relations issues. But within one day of me being with them I took over the entire role of running an HR department and I ended up completely revamping HR operations. At the time, HR was being handled by the CEO and when they realized I could do all of the HR, they gave it to me to run. This allowed the CEO to focus on the business, not on HR. In the beginning, it was a lot of cleanup from an HR operations perspective. My goals were to make all aspects operationally sound, fully utilize all the technology that was there, ensure the data was accurate and everything that was in place was compliant, and quickly identify elements that were missing.

From a culture perspective, if a company can't nail the basics, you lose credibility. Nobody wants to talk about having free lunch on Wednesdays, for example, before they have the basics of their employment contract honored. New hires need to be onboarded correctly and benefits and paychecks need to be in effect when originally communicated. When I work with a startup or any company, I always dig into this first and I refer to nailing the basics as part of Phase one of an HR, People, or Talent organization. When your employees can rely on you that the promises the company made are being delivered, then you can talk about building a culture together.

I've found, with HR-related work, that once you're involved with a company it can be like a Pandora's box because if one thing needs adjusting, so do a lot of other related components and they're all connected. I'm an all-in type of person so I don't mind doing the work to get it right.

That said, in a fractional HR role, it's important to understand what the priorities are. And sometimes after a discussion between the company and fractional HR person, the priorities change. But you want to discover that in the early stages of the assignment so everyone is aligned. Your time and resources are limited, which is why the role is fractional to begin with. Additionally, as a fractional HR person, you'll need to be flexible with what you do. While most executives are used to working at a strategic and higher level of thinking, some of the fractional roles are very hands-on and require execution. Once priorities are clear and the fractional HR person is comfortable with the skills and experience needed, a fractional role is a great short-term solution to address priorities of the leadership team.

In any job, whether it's a full-time or part-time role, you want to make sure you are aligned with the leadership team and you believe in the company's vision. These relationships and the passions for the vision will be a good foundation for success. In a fractional role you don't have a lot of time to "get onboard," you need to figure things out quickly and make an immediate, high impact.

Startup or Established?

If you have been a Chief Talent Officer or Chief Human Resources officer, then you're used to working at a very high level, but if you're working in a fractional role at a startup, you'll likely be doing a lot of execution with an eye on strategy. Typically, resources are limited, so you may be a single-person team or have someone within the organization (usually an admin) help you execute on priority or high impact tasks. As discussed earlier, a fractional HR role in a startup is usually nailing the basics, which involves a lot of execution, hands-on, roll up your sleeves kind of work. You may have to dig into the current HR operation structure, which could include partnering with a third-party HR vendor like Trinet. But you also need to keep an eye on strategy and in every action you'll need to think about how this will impact the company in 6 months or a year. Companies hire a fractional executive because they are looking for someone who does have that strategic mind and understands the big picture.

If an established company is looking for a fractional head of HR, then the situation is a little different. The fractional HR person should always be thinking about agreeing on the priorities upfront but also you'll have to answer the question, why am I here? You must understand the relationships of the leadership team and the existing HR team. You need to specifically learn about the HR team capabilities, including what everyone does and how the department manages the HR function for the company. Understanding relationships and roles are key things to figure out quickly from the beginning. Also, it's important to understand the reputation of the existing HR team and their perception internally. If your priorities are to build the HR department and make it more effective, that means you still need to dig in but you have people around you who can actually help to execute. Another key element of this role is to make sure you assess the HR talent and understand what their strengths and weaknesses are in being an effective team. And then putting a plan in place to make sure you have the right talent and experience to meet the priorities of the department.

So, not all fractional HR work is the same and the stage of the company has a big impact on the tasks that you'll do.

Transitions

Once you fulfill the priorities of the role you were hired for, a conversation needs to happen about the future. Sometimes it makes sense for the fractional HR executive to stay with the company. Other times a company will realize they don't need someone at this level yet and a solid mid-level person can handle the work for the next year or two.

One of the key reasons you'd want to use a fractional person is either to make high impact quickly for your population with someone who has a lot of experience with building and growing an HR department OR to allow a company to have access to someone with this experience at a more manageable cost. The fractional role allows the company to understand the impact of the function with limited commitment and cost. For the fractional HR executive, the benefit of being fractional is that it allows them to do what they love in a part-time capacity.

In my last role as a fractional HR executive, once it was clear they wanted me to manage the entire HR function, I created a roadmap. The first phase was all about nailing the basics and ensuring the HR operations were sound and sustainable. Phase 2 was about understanding the company's growth plan. How many people do they plan on hiring in the next 3, 6, 12 months? It also involves understanding the company more deeply and learning about the existing people, departments, job descriptions, performance review plans, compensation strategy, and other key characteristics. Phase 2 is really about understanding the company's expected growth and making sure you have the right talent to drive that. Phase 3 is discussing the future of the fractional HR role. I begin the conversations about what the leadership team needs and can afford to sustain the work that has been done. In my role, we realized that they really didn't need someone at my level. They had a more limited budget for HR and the plan I put in place was solid enough to hand over to a seasoned mid-level person who could handle the execution and build on the strategy put in place.

Qualities of a Fractional HR Person

The qualities of a successful fractional HR executive are as much about skill as they are about mindset. In a lot of cases, you need to be comfortable in self-managing and building something from nothing. Get jazzed and excited about things being messy and the desire to fix it. You need to have the comfort level and skills to actually know how to fix things yourself or manage someone to do the work. As a fractional person, in a startup environment or in an established organization, you have to have that all-in mentality like it's a full-time role, be curious and keep digging for what needs to be done, while maintaining the company priorities for hiring you. I feel all of these components absolutely need to be part of your personality, to be successful in this role.

24

CEO-to-CEO Advice About the People Role

Matt Blumberg

What comes before a full-fledged Chief People Officer? In most startups, the HR function starts out as tactical—you have to get people hired and paid—and frequently outsourced to a PEO. As the company grows, it probably in-sources payroll and benefits, hires a recruiter, and maybe has an HR Manager who handles the function.

Signs It's Time to Hire Your First Chief People Officer

You know it's time to hire a Chief People Officer when:

- You wake up in the middle of the night convinced that you're the only person in the company who cares about your core values.

- You are spending too much of your own time training managers and leaders, or working on interpersonal dynamics on your leadership team.

- Your Board asks you what your talent strategy is with respect to improving diversity, retention, and engagement metrics, while simultaneously decreasing average employee salary, and you don't have a great answer and aren't sure how to get one.

When a Fractional Chief People Officer Might Be Enough

A fractional Chief People Officer may be the way to go:

- If you have a very competent HR manager or director who has strategic inclinations but not enough experience operating as a strategic executive and who just needs a little more supervision in order to "level up."

- If you need someone to play more of a consigliere or team coach role to your executive team but don't want to engage a coach—and your day-to-day HR leader is getting the job done but is too junior to facilitate workshops for the senior team.

- If you have a very junior HR function or are in-sourcing it for the first time and need help setting up the whole function from scratch at an advanced size relative to other functions.

What Does Great Look Like in a Chief People Officer?

Ideal startup Chief People Officers do three things particularly well:

1. They believe their function is strategic. Throughout this Part of the book, Cathy writes about the ways in which HR/People can be a strategic function and not just a tactical corporate function. It's true of most functions, but for whatever reason, likely past experience, HR leaders frequently don't view themselves or their functions as strategic. If that's their frame of reference, then they will likely be tactical managers. If they

believe they can move the needle on the business by improving engagement and productivity and efficiency, if they believe they can make the executive team more effective by helping you with team facilitation and coaching ... they can do anything.

2. They call you (you, the CEO) out on things directly and firmly when they see you doing or saying anything that is a bit off, whether around language, inclusion, values, authenticity, or anything else. They along with you, are the principal stewards of the company's values and culture. Even the best CEOs benefit from having a watchdog from time to time.

3. They think about investment in People in terms of ROI. It's one thing to run a killer recruiting function and fill seats efficiently, with high quality, as asked. It's an entirely different thing to start the recruiting process by asking if the role is needed, at that level and compensation band, or whether there are other people, fractional people, contractors, or shifts in lower value activities that could be put to work instead. Only Heads of People with deep understandings of the business can transform the function from a gatekeeper/"no" role into a business accelerator.

Signs Your Chief People Officer Isn't Scaling

Chief People Officers who aren't scaling well past the startup stage are the ones who typically:

- Are overly focused on the transactional aspects of the job. Don't get me wrong, there are many transactional elements to HR—payroll, benefits, systems, process, etc.—and they all have to go well or employees freak out. But the Chief People Officer who spends all their time on these issues isn't delegating well, isn't building a machine, isn't building scalable people and processes to flawlessly and efficiently handle the details.

- Won't speak up in executive team meetings. Chief People Officers have every right and entitlement to hold opinions about the company's strategy, products, operations, and financials. The good ones do—and they're not shy about speaking up publicly about them. The weaker ones, or the ones who are in a bit over their heads, don't because they either haven't taken the time to learn and formulate those opinions, or because they don't have enough confidence among their peers, to voice them.

- Have trouble managing/leading their own team. Since a good Chief People Officer is one who spends time coaching all the other leaders in your business on how to be effective leaders, it's particularly worrisome when they themselves are not—especially with what is usually a relatively small function. This is a classic case of the cobbler's children walking around barefoot, and it's a sign of trouble for your HR leader.

How I Engage with the Chief People Officer

A few ways I've typically spent the most time or gotten the most value out of Chief People Officers over the years are:

- ALWAYS as a direct report. No matter who my HR leader is, even if the person is more junior than other executives, I will always have that person report directly to me and be part of the most senior operating group in the company. That sends the signal that the People function (and quite frankly, diversity, culture, and a whole host of other things) are just as important to me as Sales or Product.

- I insist on hearing about ALL People issues. First, I am a very "retail" CEO, and I like engaging with people in the business, at all levels, in all departments, in all locations. So I like to keep tabs on what's going on with people—who is doing particularly well and about to be promoted, who is struggling, who is a flight risk, who is going through some personal issue (good or bad) that we should know about. Even more than just me wanting to be in the know, like the example in the Weekly Sales Forecast meeting, when the Head of People knows that I want to know about all these details, they insist that all the different People Business Partners roll those issues up to them, which means they're in the know as well. The number of issues we have nipped in the bud, and the number of opportunities we've been able to jump on to help employees over the years because of this retail focus has been immense.

- As an informal coach for me and with my external coach. As I wrote in another sidebar in this Part, a great Chief People Officer can call a CEO out when a CEO needs to be called out. And that also means that great Chief People Officers engage with CEOs deeply about how they are doing, help them process difficult situations, and help them see things they might not otherwise see. Being a CEO is a lonely job sometimes, and it's good to have a People partner to be able to collaborate with on some of the most personal and sensitive issues.

- Designing and executing leadership/management training. The best way to create a multiplier effect of employee engagement and productivity in your organization is to teach all leaders and managers how to be excellent at those crafts—and how to do them in ways that are consistent with your company's values. I always took a lot of time, in large blocks of hours or days, to either co-create leadership training materials and workshops with my Head of People, or to lead sessions at those workshops and engage with the company's managers and leaders in a very personal way. That always felt to me like a very high ROI use of time.

25

Conclusion

If you can help build an organization from the startup phase, you have a unique opportunity to impact a company's DNA. Consider how all the different parts of the employee lifecycle fit together and support and reinforce each other. If you come into an organization that is in a later stage, you can still influence all these systems; it's just a little more difficult to unwind things that aren't supportive of the company values and mission. If you join a company that has significant dysfunction, which requires a lot of reactive work, insist on over-hiring for your team so you can stay focused on proactively changing the structures and systems, instead of being side-tracked dealing with difficult employee relations issues that stem from poor systems, training, and structures.

I said that I'd help you think about how to influence a CEO who isn't aligned with a people-centric approach, and there are things throughout that can help you build a business case for a people-centric approach to each body of work. The best advice I can give you is to ensure you build a trusted advisor relationship with the CEO and leadership team, and take the time to have meaningful conversations about legacy, and the impact of the different approaches to leading your employees. It's a skill that you need to hone, because we still have a cultural perspective that stems from production lines that people need to be "managed" rather than "led." Many employees are still afraid of HR and think of HR as the "police" who they have to be "politically correct" around. I wish I'd had this perspective early in my career; who knows, maybe I would have been able to influence Jerry, the truck stop president, to create a better environment for all employees if I'd had the right knowledge and skills? He was a good man who cared about his people, and just had really traditional ideas about how to manage them.

And, my final piece of advice, about which I often need reminding: take care of yourself and your team. It's so easy to be like the proverbial cobbler, whose kids didn't wear shoes. Good People professionals care about others, which is what makes them good. That often means not making time for themselves. Make sure you have an operating system where you invest as much in your own team/team members as you do in other teams. Have quarterly offsites, encourage professional development, have a good operating system so you are planful and organized about the work.

You will have a significant impact on the organization, since your team is interacting with employees at all levels. If you focus on the values, structures, and culture, and you build an environment where people can bring their whole selves to work, you can have a transformative impact on the culture and the people within it.

Acknowledgements

This book is derivative of *Startup CXO* and the acknowledgments for this book extends to the people who helped in that effort. The list of people to thank for their role in helping create that is long and has to start with my current and former colleagues who were the primary contributors: Jack Sinclair, Cathy Hawley, Shawn Nussbaum, Ken Takahashi, Nick Badgett, Holly Enneking, Anita Absey, George Bilbrey, Dennis Dayman, and Dave Wilby. *Startup CXO* was a truly collaborative work and the same is true with this book. Cathy and I collaborated together and also with Pete Birkeland, who edited the second edition of *Startup CEO*, was a tireless collaborator for *Startup CXO*, and helped bring this book to fruition.

I would also like to acknowledge the rest of the Bolster team and board that made this possible, especially this book's project manager, Rachel Henry. It wasn't easy to carve out the time to write while scaling up Bolster, much less doing the bulk of the writing over the holidays and I'm grateful to all the contributors for their effort.

Although the professional lives of the contributors are now primarily at Bolster, most of us worked together for many years at Return Path, and all of us would like to thank our Board and shareholders, particularly Fred Wilson, Greg Sands, Scott Weiss, Scott Petry, Jeff Epstein, and Brad Feld (more on Brad in a minute) for giving us the opportunity to learn on the job as we scaled ourselves and scaled the business over the better part of two decades. That experience is what led us to be able to write *Startup CXO*. We'd also like to thank all 1,300 colleagues from Return Path over the years who challenged, inspired, and taught us things every day. Although he was not a Return Path or Bolster team member, Marc Maltz from Hoola Hoop Consulting, my long-time partner as an executive coach, has shaped the thinking of me and of a number of the contributors to this effort.

Startup CXO is part of the *Startup Revolution* series that was created by my long-time board member and friend Brad Feld. Brad's advice on all things business, personal, and writing has been invaluable for over 20 years and whether attributed or not, many of the ideas in this book are the result of many thoughtful conversations with him. I would also like to thank the team at Wiley (Bill Falloon and Purvi Patel) for their help and support as editors, publishers, and marketers.

Startup CXO had a very large number of people who contributed their insights to the final form, which carries over to this book, including sidebars by Rob Krolik and Jeff Epstein, Guy Turner, Greg Sands, Scott Petry, Brad Feld, Dave Wilby, and Scott Dorsey. We are also grateful for the contribution to our fractional chapter from Courtney Graeber.

We received a number of thoughtful comments on specific functional areas from Rick Buck, Caroline Pearl, Diana Caleroni, Jen Goldman, Mike Mutone, Debby Meredith, and Chad Shinsato. Brad Feld and Scott Dorsey did a final read-through of the entire book (not a small feat!) and provided helpful suggestions to the final work.

I want to end by thanking my family for their unwavering support as I embarked on a series of books while scaling a second startup—a combination that I can't exactly endorse as being sane or smart. *Startup CXO* was a collaborative effort but I would have been the anchor holding us back if it weren't for my wife of over two decades, Mariquita. My thanks start and end with her. An executive coach for startup CEOs, Mariquita has been intimately involved in all my professional projects, providing advice, encouragement, and support to whatever I'm doing.

Matt Blumberg

About the Authors

Matt Blumberg. Matt has spent his entire career creating startups, scaling them, and sharing best practices of what works and what doesn't work for other CEOs and team members in the entrepreneurial community. He is the author of *Startup CEO: A Field Guide to Scaling Up Your Business* (Wiley, 2020), an influential book embraced by entrepreneurs, CEOs, founders, and board of directors in the entrepreneurial ecosystem. Startup CEO was an outgrowth of his blog, StartupCEO.com. In 1999, he founded Return Path, an innovative email marketing company, helped it to $100m in revenues, and led it to a successful exit in a strategic sale to Validity in 2019. Along with colleagues from Return Path, Matt started Bolster in 2020, a company focused on helping startups and scaleups grow, develop, and scale their leadership teams and boards. Matt's second book, *Startup CXO: A Field Guide to Scaling Up Your Company's Critical Functions and Teams* (Wiley, 2021), was a collaboration with Bolster's CXOs to provide a blueprint for scaling up each function.

Before Return Path, Matt led Marketing, Product Management, and the Internet Group for MovieFone, Inc. (later acquired by AOL). Prior to that, he served as an associate with private equity firm General Atlantic Partners and was a consultant with Mercer Management Consulting. He also cofounded and chairs the board of Path Forward, a nonprofit created and spun out of Return Path. Path Forward's mission is to empower people to restart their careers after time spent focused on caregiving by working with companies offering mid-career internships. Path Forward gives women and men a path to a professional career, while giving companies access to a diverse, untapped talent force. Matt is currently Executive Chair at Bolster. He earned his A.B. from Princeton University.

Cathy Hawley. Cathy is CEO of Bolster and has been an experienced fractional and full-time Chief People Officer passionate about building highly effective leadership teams and creating inclusive and people-focused workplaces. She has more than 20 years of experience in a variety of industries developing global People and Culture teams. At Return Path, she spearheaded the "return to work" program, spun it out to a nonprofit, and is on the Board of Path Forward, a nonprofit that helps companies create return-to-work programs for caregivers. Cathy contributed to *Startup CXO: A Field Guide to Scaling Up Your Company's Critical Functions and Teams* (Wiley, 2021), sharing her experience, tips, and best practices for CPOs to build a resilient culture as they scale up the People function. Cathy earned a BS in business administration from the University of Colorado and a master's in European HR and Industrial Relations from Keele University.